The NEW WINE EXPERIENCE

A Leadership Model for Church Planting in the African-American Context

By

Dr. Jermaine N. Johnson

Introduction by Bishop Claude R. Alexander, Jr

Foreword by Dr. Kenneth O. Robinson, Jr.

First Edition - First Printing

Copyright © 2014 by Jermaine N. Johnson; All rights reserved. No part of this book may be reproduced, stored in retrieval systems or transmitted in any form, electronic, mechanical, or by other means, without prior written permission from the author or publisher.

ISBN: 978-1-56411-051-0

Published by:
CB Publishing & Design
P O Box 560431
Charlotte NC 28256
(704) 390-2929
info@cbpublishing-design

Endorsements

"Dr. Jermaine N. Johnson has a deep religious and technical understanding based on years of ministerial experience combined with a rare talent for communicating important pastoral issues very simply. As a "Church Planter" and shared in "The New Wine Experience"; Dr. Johnson embodies, embraces and executes the necessary characteristics and traits required to fulfill the needs of the communities he serves; entrepreneurial, organizational, motivational as well as great communication skills. The approach he describes in "The New Wine Experience" is so fundamentally and foundationally easy to grasp-you'll see things differently and be able to lead your new church in a refreshing direction which will have a much needed favorable impact in the community."

> **JaNean Stubbs Taylor**
> **CEO & Founder, Fruits of Finance**
> **SVP, SunTrust Bank**
> **2014 Top 100 Business Women in MD.**

"Dr. Johnson offers phenomenal insight for the area of church planting in the African American context. While many pastors and church leaders have implemented many approaches to church planting in the African American context, not very many have engaged the next dimension to publish the experience and its outcomes. Dr. Johnson has entered that next dimension. The readings of this work offer a rich and spirited understanding of purpose, plan, and limitless possibilities of church planting in the African American context."

> Pastor Michelle D. Johnson, M.Div.
> **Word of Life Christian Community Church**

"Dr. Johnson's cutting edge approach in combining traditional biblical truth with new church planting methodologies sets this book apart from others. For those of us who burn and yearn to reach this generation without theological compromise, this book is our answer."

> **Dr. Kenneth O. Robinson Jr.**
> **Senior Pastor, DreamLife Worship Center**
> **Randallstown, Maryland 21133**

DEDICATION

I dedicate this accomplishment to the beloved memory of my father, Nathaniel Willis Johnson, who challenged me at a young age to memorize John 3:16.

TABLE OF CONTENTS

DEDICATION III

CHAPTER OVERVIEW VII

ACKNOWLEDGMENTS IX

ABSTRACT XI

FOREWORD XIII

INTRODUCTION XVII

    CHAPTER I: THE IDENTITY OF THE MODEL 1

    CHAPTER II: THEOLOGICAL AND BIBLICAL FRAMEWORK OF THE MODEL 21

    CHAPTER III: LITERATURE & KEY THEMES OF THE MODEL 59

    CHAPTER IV: THE DESIGN OF THE MODEL 83

    CHAPTER V: THE PRESENTATION OF THE MODEL 115

APPENDIX A: PASTORAL INTERVIEWS 131

APPENDIX B: MARKETING STRATEGIES WORKSHOP FOR THE CHURCH PLANTER 143

APPENDIX C: THE NINE FRUITS OF FINANCE 147

BIBLIOGRAPHY 155

VITA 163

CHAPTER OVERVIEW

Identity of the Model

Chapter I

Identity of the Model serves as a guide for the development and framework of establishing a culture of your ministry and/or organization. The reader is encouraged to define the terms within the context of ministry, which is a process that will provide a solid foundation for accomplishing the goal of the church and or organization.

Theological and Biblical Framework of the Model

Chapter II

The Theological and Biblical Framework chapter uses a holistic representation of the Bible that provides a comprehensive view of God's perspective on redemption. Apostles Peter and Paul's journey of redemption is outlined in this chapter, a journey that provides church planting and organizational revitalization principles. In addition, we will examine the impact that Biblical history has had on the African-American church.

Literature and Key Themes of the Model

Chapter III

The literature and key themes within this chapter are essential in the process of establishing a foundation and framework for church planting and revitalization. Hozell Francis, Michael J. Cox, Joe Samuel Ratliff and Dr. Carl Ellis represent African-American

VIII

scholarship in the context of Church Planting in the African-American community. The key themes represented in this chapter are practical and relevant attributes in the overall goal of designing and presenting a model of church planting and revitalization in the African American context of ministry.

Design of the Model

Chapter IV

The Design of the Model serves as the methodology that provides the reader with an audience, a strategic plan and encourages an atmosphere of collaboration as an approach to the conflict and tensions that surround church planting and revitalization in the context of the African American church.

Presentation of the Model

Chapter V

The Presentation of the Model provides the reader with a summary of results, which is a process that will enable the stage to be a set for an effective leadership model of church planting and revitalization in the African-American context of ministry.

ACKNOWLEDGMENTS

Thank you Jesus!

To my wonderful family and friends, who have sacrificed so much for me to have this opportunity!

My mother Vanessa Hardison, My beautiful bride Michelle, and my precious jewel Zoë. I love you all and I am forever grateful for you!

To My Word of Life Family, "It all begins with the Word, for the Word is Life!"

"Happy Birthday Zoë"

ABSTRACT

When I first discerned God's call to church planting, I wrestled with the call and attempted, like Jonah, to run. I was overcome with fears due to my limited exposure of church planting in the African-American context. There were limited resources on the subject and I was experiencing the Holy Spirit leading to plant a church in the African-American community. I witnessed a lot of successes but not of lot of successions, I witnessed personalities over philosophies of ministry. Therefore I was driven to research and develop a Redemptive Model of Leadership for Church Planting in the African-American Context.

The redemptive model of church planting in the African-American context has the potential to establish a new order that has the power to correct and build upon a legacy that has influenced and provided an identity for countless generations.

It was Jesus' mission and purpose to bring redemption and restoration: "Do not think that I came to destroy but to fulfill."

XII

Moreover, these images of cloth and wineskins in the Gospel of Mark spoke of the old coming to an end and the arrival of the new that embodied the fulfillment of the law: "The point is that the old represents old forms of Judaism which is compatible with the new, not because the old is outmodeled, but because the new packs such power that the old cannot contain it."

Foreword

"And on one puts new wine into old wineskins; or else the new wine bursts the wineskins, the wine is spilled, and the wineskins are ruined. But new wine must be put into new wineskins."
Mark 2:19-22 NKJV

    I think one of the tragedies in the African American community is not just the increased rate of fatherlessness, or the proliferation of drugs, or even the high rising unemployment rate, but rather little impact that the so many churches are having on these present-day societal ills.

    Over 20 years ago, I planted a church in an African American community and have witnessed the impact a church can have in a community. On the contrary, I have seen many churches planted that have had very little impact in their community, and eventually for one reason or another dissolved. In Dr. Gregory J. Reed's, "Economic Empowerment Through The Church, A Blueprint for Progressive Community Development," it points out that the most progressive church leadership all across the country is rethinking its priorities and networking to the commitment of serving the whole person. The culture changes of this generation has created a vacuum for a new leadership model for planting churches in a new African American context. That is why Dr. Jermaine Johnson's "The New Wine Experience, A Leadership

Model for Church Planting in the African-American Context," creates the blueprint for those who burn and yearn to reach this present generation with the gospel of our Lord Jesus Christ.

My African American church experience has been over the span of a lifetime, and I have seen the struggle of the African American church evolve in its relevancy to present day ministry. This struggle will always be present when a new order is needed to bring real life-altering change for people, families and community into wholeness. As Dr. Johnson lays out the need for a new order in church planting in this book, he also masterfully shows us how to maintain the biblical traditional truths that will help us continue to influence our present culture and build upon a legacy that will last for countless generations.

Over the years, many theologians were inevitably faced with the context of the new wine metaphor given by Christ in the gospels. *"...And on one puts new wine into old wineskins; or else the new wine bursts the wineskins, the wine is spilled, and the wineskins are ruined. But new wine must be put into new wineskins."* Mark 2:19-22 NKJV The interpretation of the text is without dispute that Christ was addressing a new order of priesthood/ ministry and perhaps even spirituality, that would fulfill the original intent of God's Law but could not be contained in the old order of the Judaism priesthood. However, very few theologians have provided a forward-thinking modern day approach for the interpretation of the text, particularly how it relates to the African American church context. In Dr. Johnson's The Wine Experience, A Leadership Model of Church Planting in the African-American Context, he provides us with the combination of a forward-thinking interpretation as well as an simple relevant application for leaders to model. As I read the context of this book, it became evident that a paradigm shift is taking place in the heart of new young African American Church Leaders such as Dr. Jermaine Johnson, who love the message of the gospel of Christ but are striving to find new cutting-edge strategies that will capture the hearts of a lost and dying generation. Church planting is simply fulfilling the mandate of Jesus Christ's ministry when He said "for the Son of Man has come to seek and to save that which was lost." (Luke 19:10 NKJV) This is a handbook to educate, empower and equip any church leader, pastor or minister on how to fulfill this mandate in our generation with excellence and efficiency. Although some of these strategies and models are not included in seminary courses, yet Dr. Johnson has intricately interwoven his own unique church planting experience and seminary knowledge to create the volumes of wisdom captured in this book. Also, as a pastor and author myself, I appreciate the direct transformational style of presentation in which he writes.

This volume should go a long way in answering the questions and applying the answers needed for church leaders to plant churches in our present generation.

Dr. Kenneth O. Robinson Jr., MDiv., MCEP
Sr. Pastor of DreamLife Worship Center
Founder of Kingspoint Fellowship Network
Randallstown, Maryland

Introduction

The progress of the Christian Church throughout time has been built upon its consistency and its adaptability. The consistency of the Church is rooted in the core conviction that Jesus is the Christ, the Son of the Living God, who died for our sins according to the scriptures, was buried, and was raised from the dead according to the scriptures.

These core convictions anchor the Church. Yet throughout the history of the Church, there has been a need for adaptability in terms of form and structure. To accommodate the demands brought about by the rapid growth of the early church, the structure of the Church adapted with formation of the diaconate. In response to the resistance within the temple and synagogues, believers went from house to house. In concert with the flow of God's movement, the epicenter of the church moved from Jerusalem to Antioch, and later to Ephesus.

At its best, the Church is both settled and fluid. It is settled by its core convictions while being fluid in terms of its modalities and expressions.

In his book The New Wine Experience, Dr. Jermaine Johnson insightfully explores this in terms of church planting. While church planting is nothing new to scripture, it is a relatively new approach in the African-American context. The times in which we live provide a significant opportunity for pastors and churches to expand the redemptive reach of Christ through a sound approach to church planting that highlights the settled and fluid nature of the Church. The New Wine Experience provides a redemptive approach to church planting that enables the reader to rise to the opportunity.

Bishop Claude R. Alexander, Jr.
The Park Church
Charlotte, NC

CHAPTER I

THE IDENTITY OF THE MODEL

Purpose

The purpose of this book is to formulate a comprehensive Redemptive Leadership model for church planters in the African-American context. This project will examine the elements that are necessary for an effective developmental model that meets the needs of African-American men and women seeking to plant churches in the African-American context of ministry. Church planting in the African-American context may be considered by some as an oxymoron due to the fact that there are still some major reservations in the African-American community to the concept. According to Ed Stetzer, author of *Planting Missional Churches*, "Others see church planting as a waste of valuable time and money, resources that could be used to revitalize declining churches while others see church planters as merely a way of stealing members from nearby churches."[1]

Many in the African-American community hold the sentiments expressed by Stetzer. As a result they are reluctant to fully embrace the ideology that comes with church planting. The major question they have is, "What does church planting represent that the established church doesn't?" The world is changing, and as a result people are changing. The world has become such a diverse place through gentrification, which is changing the spectrum of our communities. Coupled with these developments, one can see how church planting in the African-American community is considered a threat to the historical significance of the African-American church. Dr. Gardner Taylor writes,

Our culture is a given; we are all children and products of it. But having said that, culture is not a prison. It does not have to restrict us; it does have to circumscribe us. If the gospel is not able to get us beyond our culture, it is not a gospel at all, because there is no pure gospel in any one culture. It does not matter if the good news of the

---

[1] Ed Stetzer, *Planting Missional Churches* (Nashville, TN: Broadman & Holman, 2006), 5.

gospel is bad news in the culture. We are not owned by our culture; it is a secondary identity over which we rank the demands of God.[2]

The words of Dr. Taylor serve as a bridge that the African-American church needs in order to embrace the ideology that the redemptive model has to offer. As a result, I believe that church planting serves as a catalyst in providing fresh perspective and insight that will equip and empower the African-American church and community to engage the pluralistic culture around it.

As disciples we must always remember the mandate of the Great Commission to go and make disciples. This was the ethos of the African-American churches that began in small groups, where the passion for fulfilling the Great Commission, worship, and liberation took on a life of its own. The original church plant never focused on numbers, but rather it was moved by substance, purpose, agenda, and common interest. As a result, there is much relevance and significance in the traditional style of worship that needs to transcend generations and culture. I will argue that the

---

[2] Samuel D. Proctor and Gardner C. Taylor, *We Have This Ministry* (Valley Forge, PA: Judson Press, 1996), 5.

vehicle for these principles resides in a redemptive model of church planting in the African-American context of ministry. The redemptive model that we subscribe to consists of five stages: competency, principles, character, transformation, and redemption. For the purpose of advancing the gospel of Jesus Christ, these stages are an essential guide for leadership and development.

Practical Relevance

The first stage of the redemptive model is competency. This principle is paramount to beginning the redemptive process for the empowerment of a group or organization. Candace Lewis of Path One, a United Methodist Church planter provides us with a process of practical relevance with her research, *Things to Consider in New Church Planting in the African-American Context:*

Pastors of new black churches should be entrepreneurial and have great organizational, motivational and communication skills.

Additionally, they must possess a clear vision for what the impact of the new church will mean to the community they must have a clear understanding of United Methodist requirements around new church planting they must be able to network with other successful planters across denominational lines.[3]

Moreover, there is a need for effective ministry in our urban contexts, so a strategic plan must be welcomed and implemented. Ed Stetzer writes, One out of every six churches in North America is African-American, yet the number of unchurched African-Americans is constantly rising. The need for planting new churches in African-American communities intensifies every year, especially in light of the gradual erosion of interest in traditional worship styles among African-American young adults.[4] This statement is a hard truth, which we must confront as pastors and

---

[3] Candace Lewis, "Things to Consider in New Church Planting in African American Context," accessed November, 14, 2013, http://www.path1.org/images/File/AA%20Church%20planting%20best%20practices%2006_07_10.pdf, 1.

[4] Stetzer, *Planting Missional Churches*, 120.

leaders in our African-American churches and communities. We must have a mandate to reproduce, by telling and living out the story through the gospel of Jesus Christ. According to Gary McIntosh, author of *One Church, Four Generations*, the challenge facing today's church is simultaneous and effective ministry to people of four widely divergent generations. More than at any time in history, pastors must plan programs that will appeal to a mosaic of groups and subgroups. The youngest generation, entitled "the bridges," is perhaps the most difficult one to reach for Christ. The characteristics, interests, and values of each group (Builders, Boomers, Busters, and Bridgers) are explored in relation to the historical events and social trends that have shaped them."[5]

Furthermore, while researching the subject of African-American church planting, there seemed to be limited resources in regards to scholarship. The most recent publication was written by Hozell C. Francis entitled, *Church Planting in the African-*

---

[5] Gary McIntosh, *One Church, Four Generations: Understanding and Reaching All Ages in Your Church* (Grand Rapids, MI: Baker Books, 2002), Back Cover.

American Context. Ed Stetzer challenged me to my core when he wrote in reference to this subject, "I would welcome more scholarship on this vital subject from church planting experts and authors who have personal experience to share."[6]

Theological Importance

At its core, church planting is a unique ministry opportunity that has the capacity to yield an equipping model of ministry for the body of Christ. The process of church planting is driven by a fundamental understanding of its purpose to customize the journey of discipleship. Throughout the Gospels and the New Testament writings, kingdom principles are outlined and designed for followers of Jesus Christ to be direct and intentional in our pursuit of fulfilling the Great Commission. When the correlation of principles are comprehended and followed, we as believers are positioned to yield a harvest of fruitful production.

According to the gospel of Matthew, as Jesus is mentoring

---

[6] Stetzer, *Planting Missional Churches*, 121.

and developing his disciples for future church planting opportunities, he takes a moment to ask a fundamental question, "Who do men say that I am?"[7] This question is of great theological significance because it is a question of identity. This is the second stage of the redemptive model.

The question of identity is key to the process of presenting a model of redemptive church planting in the African-American context of ministry, primarily due to the culture's identity crisis that has such a strong historical and theological significance. Identity is a contributing factor whenever one's engaging in the process of redemption. Identity defines and articulates your character. According to Major Jones, author of the *The Color of God*, "Black Theology expresses a new light of freedom under God, the Black person, locked in the struggle for liberation, will stop at nothing short of expressing both in act and being an ever stronger

---

[7] Matthew 16:13-18 NKJV

affirmation of Black selfhood."[8] In addition Jones writes, "Black Theology often becomes that truth which places a Black person for the first time in touch with a deep core of themselves; and once a person finds that core meaning of selfhood, he or she is prepared to give all for it, which is the ultimate liberation intent of Black Theology."[9]

The issues surrounding identity, redemption, culture, history, theology, and church planting are rooted in a myriad of emotions and theories, therefore the question which Jesus asked his disciples is paramount if there's hope for liberation and redemption. Dr. Carl Ellis, Jr. writes,

We all have core concerns life defining and life controlling values and or issues. These concerns can be personal, social and or cultural, yet the cultural core concerns distinguish people groups. Generally, the societal norms and protocols are oriented to the dominant culture. Because, of this, the cultural core concerns of the sub-dominant culture tend to be left unaddressed. In the African

---

[8] Major Jones, *The Color of God: The Concept of God in Afro-American Thought* (Macon, GA: Mercer University Press, 1990), 5.

[9] Jones, *The Color of God*, 5.

American culture, these concerns are related to empowerment, namely, dignity, identity, and significance.[10]

Statement of the Problem and Researchable Question

According to Hozell C. Francis, author of *Church Planting in the African-American Context,* "The motivation for planting a new church should be considered with extreme carefulness. There are a number of factors that must be pondered, not the least of which is whether a call to church planting is evident."[11] Moreover, Francis writes,

> One in every six churches in the United States is African American. So, given the church's central role in the black community why is the number of unchurched African-Americans increasing? How can you plant a church that

---

[10] *African-American Church Planting Research Report,* LifeWay Research, last modified July 15, 2013, accessed November 10, 2013, http://pcamna.org/wordpress/wp-content/uploads/2013/08/African-American-Church-Planting-Final-Quantitative-Research-Report.pdf, 8.

[11] Hozell C. Francis, *Church Planting in the African-American Context* (Grand Rapids, MI: Zondervan Publishing House, 1999), 25.

proclaims with power and relevance the unchanging gospel to our changing African-American culture?[12]

As a result, the topic will develop and answer the question, How can Church planting in the African-American context use the redemptive model for the further development of the African-American church? The question assumes the African-American church wants to experience a new model with a redemptive focus that will aide in enriching and reclaiming its legacy and traditions across generational and denominational lines.

Structure of the Study/Methodology

The methodology of this research is based on a seminar designed to provide church planters with a forum to discuss their processes and the relevancy of using the redemptive model in the African-American church and community through church planting. The researcher's hope is for the church planter to see how the principles of church planting can aide in the overall

---

[12] Francis, *Church Planting in the African-American Context,* Back Cover.

impact of the church. The process affords the opportunity for discussion and exposure to different ideologies and concepts that are beneficial to the ongoing development of the church. Pastors who participated in the process were from a non-denominational background with Methodist experience, who has had experience planting churches in the African-American context.

Research and Hypothesis Goals

The research for this project is designed to lead toward intentionally formulating a process using the redemptive model that will incorporate the principles of church planting. Church planting is a redemptive work that has the ability to impact cultures and communities. The question before us is, Can church planting using a redemptive model be effective within the African-American Church? There are several questions that we will ask that will aid us in drawing our conclusion. In addition to the questions we have conducted several case studies among African-

American church planters.[13] In addition to the case studies, three pastors who have planted churches participated in interviews and completed questionnaires. Our goal is to present the results from the qualitative interviews that would benefit African-American church planters.

Glossary of Terms

The following list of terms has been defined for the reader. Dr. Rodney L. Cooper's lecture notes on the redemptive model will be adopted throughout the framework for subscribing to the redemptive model.

---

[13] "Case studies are the preferred strategy when 'how' or why' questions are being posed, when the investigator has little control over the event, and when the focus is on a contemporary phenomenon within some real-life context." Robert Yin, *Case Study Research: Design and Methods* (Thousand Oaks, CA: Sage Publications, 2003), 1.

Redemptive Model

The redemptive model serves as a guide that provides the opportunity for reflection, restoration, and revitalization. The contents of the model consist of five stages:

1. Competency = skill and ability
2. Principles = a fundamental quality or attribute
3. Character = strength and originality of a person's nature
4. Transformation = a dramatic change in appearance
5. Redemptive = making something better or more acceptable

Traditional African-American Church

A religious organization in the African-American community that has established a strong presence, based on stability, symbols and cultural themes and artifacts that have been commonly associated with the African-American Church. These associations include, houses of worship, church attire, rhetoric, styles of preaching, music, etc.

Church Planting in the African-American Context

The establishment of a newly organized religious institution among a specified culture and community.

Redemption

Serves as the stimulation and compass of discussion and direction for the life and future of the African-American Church.

Assumptions

Church planting is a divinely ordained work that must be directed and guided by God. The role of the Holy Spirit is implied throughout this project. The attributes and ministry of the Holy Spirit must be acknowledged while embracing the assignment of church planting; however, few Christian authors ever mention his work in connection to this ministry. Gary McIntosh writes,

It is the life-giving work of the Holy Spirit that empowers church programs, plans, and strategies. Churches that rely solely on human personality and ingenuity may grow for a time, but their growth will have little spiritual weight beneath the surface.

This is because some churches rely too heavily on human analysis and projections.[14]

The authority and inspiration of Scripture is assumed. The Word of God is the foundation of the church: "All scripture is inspired by God and is useful for teaching, for reproof, for correction, and for training in righteousness, so that everyone who belongs to God may be proficient, equipped for every good work."[15]

Parameters of the Project

The substance of this journey is a comprehensive analysis of those who have been called to church planting in the African-American context. A church that has its foundation built upon biblical authority, sound doctrine, and the ability to be culturally relevant will have a significant impact on the redemptive work

---

[14] Gary L. McIntosh, *Biblical Church Growth: How You Can Work with God to Build a Faithful Church* (Grand Rapids, MI: Baker Books, 2003), 85.

[15] 2 Timothy 3:16-17 NRSV

within the culture, community, and moreover the church. The goal is to establish a culture of leadership within the context of the African-American community that will provide future generations with further research opportunities that can later be applied to specific areas related to this topic.

Chapter I describes the preliminary problem and its setting and furthermore serves as a guide for the ongoing development and answer to our research questions. In addition, it provides the broad outline of a framework needed to pursue and assess the research question.

Chapter II invites the biblical and theological framework into the discussion of church planting. Before we can proceed with attempting to redeem the church, we must start with the Bible and constitute a theological framework. Our intent is to use a holistic representation of the Old and New Testament Scriptures that will provide us with a comprehensive view of God's perspective on redemption. In addition, we will examine the impact that Biblical history has had on the African-American Church.

Chapter III serves as a literature review. The literature in the field of church planting and leadership were very relevant. Various authors illuminated the subject of redemption through church planting. There was a limited representation from the African-American community in the form and literature of church planting in the African-American context. However those that did contribute, have made a significant impact in the development of this project.

Chapter IV describes the methods of research related to the process of developing a model for redeeming the African-American church through church planting. The methodology provides us, as an audience, a strategic plan and encourages an atmosphere of collaboration as an approach to the conflict and tensions that surround redemptive church planting in the context of African-American ministries.

Chapter V provides a summation of our anticipated results, a process that will enable us to set the stage for an effective model of redemptive leadership in the African-American context of ministry. In addition, we will make recommendations for further research that would provide greater depth and scope than is possible in this project.

The bibliography catalogues the literature that informed this project and its contents. It includes books, periodical articles, and content in electronic formats that formed a framework for this project.

The appendices will include material from the research such as interviews, source documents, surveys, questionnaires, and a marketing strategy for the church planter.

CHAPTER II

THEOLOGICAL AND BIBLICAL FRAMEWORK OF THE MODEL

Introduction

The theological foundation for providing a redemptive model for the African-American church through church planting is based on the person and work of Jesus Christ. Throughout the Gospels, Jesus spoke to uprooting only to build anew. In the Gospel according to Mark, Jesus and the Pharisees have a discussion concerning fasting, which amounts to a conflict between an old system that is broken and a new order that has the power to fix it. The disciples of John and the Pharisees had questions and concerns about Jesus' teachings, due to the fact that they were contrary to their traditions:

"Why do the disciples of John and of the Pharisees fast, but Your disciples do not fast?" And Jesus said to them, "Can the friends of the bridegroom fast while the bridegroom is with them? As long as they have the bridegroom with them they cannot fast. But the days will come when the bridegroom will be taken away from them, and then they will fast in those days. No one sews a piece of unshrunk cloth on an old garment; or else the new piece pulls away from the old, and the tear is made worse. And no one puts new wine into old wineskins; or else the new wine bursts the wineskins, the wine is spilled, and the wineskins are ruined. But new wine must be put into new wineskins."[1]

The question was asked out of passion and concern for the law a system that was in desperate need of reconstruction. It was Jesus' mission and purpose to bring redemption and restoration: "Do not think that I came to destroy the Law or the Prophets. I did not come to destroy but to fulfill."[2] Moreover, these images of

---

[1] Mark 2:19-22 NKJV
[2] Matthew 5:17 NKJV

cloth and wineskins in the Gospel of Mark spoke of the old coming to an end and the arrival of the new that embodied the fulfillment of the law: "The point is that the old represents old forms of Judaism which is compatible with the new, not because the old is outmodeled, but because the new packs such power that the old cannot contain it."[3] This parable shares similar tensions within the African-American church and community. The African-American church has been a bedrock for the African-American community and culture for more than three centuries. The African-American church over the years has symbolized hope, opportunity, and equality: "Talented black men and women developed their leadership skills in black churches and used them as launching pads for professional careers in the church or elsewhere in black society like education, music, and entertainment.[4] However, as a

---

[3] Clinton E. Arnold, ed., *Zondervan Illustrated Bible Background Commentary*, vol.1, *Matthew, Mark, Luke*, (Grand Rapids, MI: Zondervan, 2002), 223.

[4] C. Eric Lincoln and Lawrence H. Mamiya, *The Black Church in the African American Experience* (Durham, NC: Duke University Press, 1990), 383.

result of the opportunities that have been made by the African-American Church, "there is some evidence that the present and past central importance of the Black Church may be threatened by the virtual explosion of opportunities."[5] As a result, this threat and many other variables that are significant—such as a lack of evangelism, secularization, and a lack of development among younger generations—has caused a decline in the influence and impact of the African-American church. Therefore, the African-American church is ready for a redemptive process that is modeled through the work of church planters who embody principles that are relevant and engaging across generational lines. The redemptive model of church planting in the African-American context has the potential to establish a new order that has the power to correct and build upon a legacy that has influenced and provided an identity for countless generations.

---

[5] Lincoln and Mamiya, *The Black Church in the African American Experience*, 383.

As we proceed to establish a biblical and theological framework, our intent is to use a holistic approach to Scripture that will provide a more comprehensive view of God's perspective on redeeming creation; and we will look at the impact that biblical history has had on the African-American church. Jesus provided a great example by affirming the gifts of the disciples as He mentored and discipled them for three and a half years. Following the ascension of Jesus, the disciples scattered in different directions to plant churches in a variety of contexts. In this study, Scripture will serve as an archetype to the notion of redemption in the form of church planting.

Theological Motivation

Dr. Stephen Boyer of Eastern University taught one of the greatest and most impactful classes of my academic journey. The class was entitled "Theological Thinking." This class was my introduction to theology and deepened my focus and understanding of the body of Christian Doctrine.[6] So I am convinced that the church planter must be equipped with sound doctrine that is based on a biblical framework—framework that is rooted in Scripture, and is set on fulfilling the commands of Jesus and the greater purpose of the Church.

In the context of African-American church planting, there lives an ongoing debate on whether there should be an African-American church. However the African-American church is a significant part of the identity of the culture. Dr. Carl Ellis Jr. writes, "in the African American culture, the concerns are related to empowerment, namely, dignity, identity and significance."[7]

---

[6] "Doctrine deals with general or timeless truths about God and the rest of reality. It is not simply the study of specific historical events, such as what God has done, but of the very nature of the God who acts in history." Millard J. Erickson, *Introducing Christian Doctrine* (Grand Rapids, MI: Baker Academic, 2001), 16.

[7] *African-American Church Planting Research Report*, LifeWay Research, last modified July 15, 2013, accessed November 10, 2013, http://pcamna.org/wordpress/wp-content/uploads/2013/08/African-American-Church-Planting-Final-Quantitative-Research-Report.pdf, 8.

Similarly, Lincoln and Mamiya argue that "probably the most crucial of all concerns is the need to bolster the personal and cultural identity and the self-esteem of black youngsters at all socioeconomic levels."[8]

Dr. Carl Ellis, Jr. also provides us a summary of the historical significance of the 19th and 20th century culture of the African-American church:

African American theology emerged during the antebellum period. In the South, this theology was a theology of suffering because of the stresses of slavery. It was also intuitive because Blacks in the South were denied access to formal education. In the North, the theology was more cognitively oriented because northern Blacks had greater access to formal education. Like its southern counterpart, the northern theology addressed salvation by grace through faith in Christ, etc., however the two differed in one fundamental aspect; the northern theology adequately addressed empowerment core concerns, whereas southern

---

[8] Lincoln and Mamiya, *The Black Church in the African American Experience*, 402.

theology did not.

"With the end of slavery, the southern church began to adopt the northern empowerment theology. As a result, between 1870 and 1910 the African American church experienced explosive growth. However the stresses of the late 19th Century, namely, the Jim Crow practices and terrorism of the post-Reconstruction South, caused the southern church to turn inward and revert to the old intuitive theology."[9]

By the end of the 19th century, much of the northern theological tradition was eventually undercut by humanistic heresies. This rendered these cognitively oriented churches powerless and non-transformative. Without a prophetic voice, many churches of this tradition ended up degenerating into mere sociological institutions or political bases. Thus, African-American cultural core concerns were no longer addressed.

The situation did not improve in the 20th century as Dr. Ellis goes on to argue:

---

[9] *African-American Church Planting Research Report.*

The story of 20th Century African American culture can be told in terms of attempts to bridge this growing gap with alternative theologies and ideologies, e.g., the Garvey Movement, several Black Nationalist Islamic sects, the Harlem Renaissance and Black Consciousness, to name a few. By the end of the 20th Century, it was apparent that all these non-Christian attempts to adequately address African American cultural core concerns had fallen short. In the wake of this failure has emerged a creeping cultural crisis mainly seen in the rise of nihilism and the loss of identity.[10]

Lincoln and Mamiya similarly stress the importance of this crisis: "Above all, cultural identity and self-esteem are affected most significantly."[11]

Biblical Motivation

Throughout the Gospels and the New Testament writings,

---

[10] *African-American Church Planting Research Report.*
[11] Lincoln and Mamiya. *The Black Church in the African American Experience*, 403.

church planting has had an emerging presence. The historical book of Acts is the book most associated with church planting, due to the early work of the Apostles and later the establishment of churches under the direction of the Apostle Paul. The Apostle Paul embodied the Redemptive model as a result of a personal encounter with Jesus that lead to a time of reflection, restoration, and revitalization;

Now Saul was consenting to his death. At that time a great persecution arose against the church which was at Jerusalem; and they were all scattered throughout the regions of Judea and Samaria, except the apostles. And devout men carried Stephen to his burial, and made great lamentation over him. As for Saul, he made havoc of the church, entering every house, and dragging off men and women, committing them to prison."[12]

Saul's hatred toward the church continued until he journeyed on the road to Damascus and was met with a sudden light from heaven;
"Then Saul, still breathing threats and murder against the disciples of the Lord, went to the high priest and asked letters from him to

---

[12] Acts 8:1-3 NKJV

the synagogues of Damascus, so that if he found any who were of the Way, whether men or women, he might bring them bound to Jerusalem. As he journeyed he came near Damascus, and suddenly a light shone around him from heaven. Then he fell to the ground, and heard a voice saying to him, "Saul, Saul, why are you persecuting Me?" And he said, "Who are You, Lord?" Then the Lord said, "I am Jesus, whom you are persecuting. It is hard for you to kick against the goads." So he, trembling and astonished, said, "Lord, what do You want me to do?" Then the Lord said to him, "Arise and go into the city, and you will be told what you must do." And the men who journeyed with him stood speechless, hearing a voice but seeing no one. Then Saul arose from the ground, and when his eyes were opened he saw no one. But they led him by the hand and brought him into Damascus.[13]

This encounter with Jesus changed the compass of Saul's life (Saul's name would later be changed to Paul). Moreover, this encounter between Jesus and Paul is a direct reflection of the stages of the redemptive model, a model that consists of competency, principles, character, transformation, and redemption. As a result of Paul's transformation, he would later become an Apostle, a leader of the church and was credited with writing over two thirds of the New Testament. Oswald Chambers

---

[13] Acts 9:1-8 NKJV

writes, "the humility Paul manifests was produced in him by the remembrance that Jesus, whom he had scorned and despised, whose followers he had persecuted, whose Church he had harried, not only had forgiven him, but made him His chief apostle."[14] As a result of Paul's experience, he was commonly identified throughout the book of Acts with church planting among specified communities and various cultural groups.

Therefore, Ed Stetzer develops a biblical model of the church planter based on the Apostle Paul's attributes and a biblical model of the church plant based on the Book of Acts. These models are essential in establishing a culture of church planting in the African-American context of ministry.

Paul the Planter
1) Paul was personally prepared for his church-planting ministry
    a. His world-class formal training gave him a broad understanding of divine history.
    b. He was vitally connected with God (2 Corinthians 12:7-9).

---

[14] Oswald Chambers, *Growing Deeper with God* (Ann Arbor, MI: Servant Publications, 1997), 71.

c. He became prepared by stepping out in ministry from the start (Acts 9:20-22).
d. He was teachable. He apprenticed under Barnabas. He was willing to be under authority before God put him over others (Acts 11:25-26).
e. He lived an exemplary life (I Thessalonians 2).

2) Paul was an evangelist
   a. He began preaching the gospel right after conversion (Acts 9:19-22).
   b. He was a net fisherman in two ways: he led whole families to Christ (Acts 16:25-33), and he conducted large-group evangelistic meetings (Acts 13:44; 14:1).
   c. He looked for those who were most receptive (Acts 18:6).

3) Paul was an entrepreneurial leader
   a. He had vision and call from God (Acts 9:15; Romans 15:20-23).
   b. His vision was to be the apostle to the Gentiles by leading missionary teams into new territories to plant churches. He combined quick-strike evangelism with church planting.
   c. He selected the workers and apprentices he wanted on his team. He was not afraid to ask others to make sacrifices for the cause of Christ (Acts 16:2-3). Sometimes he would not let people on his team (Acts 15:38). Paul also appointed long-term leaders for the churches he started (Acts 14:23). He gave direction to

           his teammates as to where they should minister (Acts 18:19; 19-22)
      d. He received direction from God as to where his team should plant, and his teammates had confidence in his decisions (Acts 16:6-10).
      e. He was a proactive strategist (Acts 13:14, 44-49). He established a reproducible pattern for his church planting (Acts 14:1; 17:2).
      f. He deliberately did advanced planning (Acts 19:21).

4) Paul was a team player
      a. He was willing to be on a team (Acts 13:1-5).
      b. He always planted with a team (Acts 15:40; Acts 16:6; 20:4).
      c. He had a sending base church to which he reported back (Acts 14:26-28).

5) Paul was a flexible, risk-taking pioneer (I Corinthians 9:19-21)
      a. He constantly penetrated new territory (Romans 15:20).
      b. He targeted a new group (Romans 11:1).
      c. He pioneered new methods of ministry (Acts 13).

6) Paul cared for people (Role of the Shepherd)
      a. He invested personally in the lives of others (Acts 20:31).
      b. He was like a nursing mother and encouraging father (I Thessalonians 2:7-11).
      c. He was vitally concerned with the growth and development of converts (Acts 14:22).
      d. He drew close to coworkers (2 Timothy 1:2).

7) Paul empowered others (Role of the Equipper)
   a. In order to lead this rapidly growing movement, he risked delegation to young Christians (Acts 16:1-3).
   b. His team planted churches on their first missionary journey and then a few months later came back to these new churches and appointed elders (Acts 13:13, 21; 14:21-23).
   c. He recognized his own strengths and weaknesses and delegated to others according to their strengths (Titus 1:5).
8) Paul stayed committed to fulfilling God's calling and vision even at the cost of extreme personal sacrifice (Acts 14:19-20; 2 Corinthians 11:23-28).
   a. He never backed down, and he never gave up.
   b. He maintained a thankful attitude in the face of cruel and unfair treatment (Acts 16:25).
9) Paul was willing to let go of his church plants and move on to plant more (Acts 16:40)
   a. It seems that Paul needed special encouragement to stay in a city for very long (Acts 18:9-11).
   b. The longest he ever stayed in any one place was three years (Acts 20:31).
   c. Ephesus was possibly his strongest plant and our best model (Acts 19:10).
   d. He had faith in God's ability to keep the churches he started strong (Acts 20:32).

- e. He was willing to let his best teammates leave his team in order to benefit the kingdom of God best (Acts 17:14).
- f. He followed the example of Barnabas, who was willing to let go of the top position on the church planting team (Acts 13:6-12).
- g. He modeled the church at Antioch that was willing to let go of its top leaders (Acts 13:1-4).[15]

The Apostle was a missionary at heart, as he embodied and exhibited a passion for change and empowerment within the faith community. The New Testament writings of the Apostle Paul demonstrate for us his desire to fulfill the command of Jesus. Furthermore, according to Stetzer, "Identifying the values and actions of Paul can enrich the ministry of every modern-day church planter."[16] The Book of Acts establishes for us a model for church planting:

Therefore, when they had come together, they asked Him, saying, "Lord, will You at this time restore the kingdom to Israel?" And He said to them, "It is not for you to know times or seasons which the

---

[15] Ed Stetzer, *Planting Missional Churches* (Nashville, TN: Broadman & Holman, 2006), 45-47.

[16] Stetzer, *Planting Missional Churches*, 34.

Father has put in His own authority. But you shall receive power when the Holy Spirit has come upon you; and you shall be witness to Me in Jerusalem, and in all Judea and Samaria, and to the end of the earth."[17]

This encounter between the Resurrected Jesus and the future Apostles of the church, established the groundwork for missionary service throughout the Book of Acts. This missionary work would evolve into the establishment of the church—an establishment that provides us a solid model and framework to carry out the instructions of Christ and further the ongoing work of the church. According to Stetzer, "the book of Acts is the most important book ever written on the subject."[18]

Church Planting in the Book of Acts
1) Church Planting in Jerusalem (Acts 1-7)
    a) Its Origin
        i) Born in Prayer (1:12-14)
        ii) Bathed in the Spirit (2:1-4)
        iii) Begun with proclamation (2:14-39)
        iv) Baptized in the name of Jesus (2:41)

---

[17] Acts 1:6-8 NKJV

[18] Stetzer, *Planting Missional Churches*, 44.

b) Its Functions
      i) Doctrinal Teaching (2:42)
      ii) Fellowship (2:42)
      iii) Worship (2:42,46)
      iv) Prayer (2:42; 4:29-31)
      v) Benevolence (2:44-45; 4:34-35)
      vi) Identification with the Community (2:47)
      vii) Witness (4:33; 5:42)
   c) Its Growth
      i) Three thousand baptized at Pentecost (2:41)
      ii) People saved daily (2:47)
      iii) Two thousand saved on Solomon's Portico (4:4)
      iv) Multitudes added (5:14)
      v) Priests believe (6:7)
   d) Its Organization
      i) Apostles (6:2)
      ii) Deacons (6:3)
      iii) Congregation (6:5)
      iv) Elders (15:6, 22)
2) Church Planting in Judea and Samaria (Acts 8-12)
   a) Church Planting done by laity (8:1, 4)
   b) Mass evangelism (8:5-6, 12)
   c) Village evangelism (8:25)
   d) Churches multiplied (9:31)
   e) Salvation extended to Gentiles (10:44-48)[19]

---

[19] Stetzer, *Planting Missional Churches*, 48-49.

At this point in the journey, the church is building off the momentum of the commands of Jesus in Acts 1. The church has been empowered, has empowered others, has organizational structure in place, and now finds itself in the position to take the gospel to the uttermost parts of the world. This is the intersection that precedes the founding of the church in Antioch. "The founding of the Antioch church may be the most important moment in church planting history. Antioch would send missionaries throughout the entire world."[20]

3) Church Planting in the World (Acts 13-28)
   a) Scattered laity started Jewish churches (11:19)
   b) Christians from Jerusalem plant Gentile- Jewish church in Antioch (11:20-21)
   c) Antioch became the great missionary church
      i) Sensitive to the Holy Spirit (13:2)
      ii) Submissive to the Spirit (13:3)
      iii) Sending Church (13:3)
   d) Paul's First Missionary Journey (13-14)
      i) Preached first in synagogues (13:5; 14:1)
      ii) Shifted to the Gentiles (13:46)
      iii) Moved from city to city (13:13-14)
      iv) Appointed elders to lead the churches (14:23)

---

[20] Stetzer, *Planting Missional Churches*, 50.

        v) Returned to check on the new churches (14:21)
- e) Paul's Second Missionary Journey (15:40-18:22)
    - i) Employed a team ministry (15:40)
    - ii) Returned to visit new churches (15:41)
    - iii) Guided by the Holy Spirit (16:9-10)
    - iv) Evangelized households (16:15, 33)
    - v) Taught in the marketplace (17:17)
    - vi) Contextualized the message (17:22-23)
    - vii) Emphasized responsive peoples (18:6)
- f) Paul's Third Missionary Journey (18:23-21:17)
    - i) Returned to visit the churches (18:23)
    - ii) Established mother churches in urban areas (19:10; I Thessalonians 1:8)
    - iii) Started house churches (20:20)
    - iv) Encouraged stewardship in new churches (I Corinthians 16:1-3)[21]

The journey of church planting throughout the book of Acts begin with the commands of Jesus, and was carried out by a myriad of New Testament followers, most notably the Apostle Paul. He modeled for us the necessity of the redemptive work of church planting among faith communities. Paul's model provides insight and instruction to the redemptive work of church planting

---

[21] Stetzer, *Planting Missional Churches*, 49.

in the African-American context: "Any church wishing to rediscover the dynamic nature of the early church should consider planting new churches."[22]

In addition to the contribution the Apostle Paul made on to the subject of church planting in the book of Acts, the Apostle Peter played a significant role as well in the development of the church. Acts chapters 1-12 outlines for us the impact that Peter's leadership had on the establishment and the expansion of the church. Both Paul and Peter's life embodied the redemptive model as they both encountered a dramatic transformation with Jesus that can be articulated through the lense of the redemptive model.

The Call of Peter

In discerning church planting in the African-American context, Jesus' interaction with Peter in the Gospel of Luke speaks volumes to the depth of preparation needed for the assignment:

So it was, as the multitude pressed about Him to hear the word of God, that He stood by the Lake of Gennesaret, and saw two boats standing by the lake; but the fishermen had gone from them and

---

[22] Stetzer, *Planting Missional Churches*, 52.

were washing their nets. Then He got into one of the boats, which was Simon's, and asked him to put out a little from the land. And He sat down and taught the multitudes from the boat. When He had stopped speaking, He said to Simon, "Launch out into the deep and let down your nets for a catch." But Simon answered and said to Him, "Master, we have toiled all night and caught nothing; nevertheless at Your word I will let down the net." And when they had done this, they caught a great number of fish, and their net was breaking. So they signaled to their partners in the other boat to come and help them. And they came and filled both the boats, so that they began to sink. When Simon Peter saw it, he fell down at Jesus' knees, saying, "Depart from me, for I am a sinful man, O Lord!" For he and all who were with him were astonished at the catch of fish which they had taken; and so also were James and John, the sons of Zebedee, who were partners with Simon. And Jesus said to Simon, "Do not be afraid. From now on you will catch men." So when they had brought their boats to land, they forsook all and followed Him.[23]

Peter's journey of discipleship began with Jesus in Luke 5, and in this chapter Peter experiences all five stages of the redemptive process as he was challenged and empowered to become the future leader of the church.

According to this narrative, the stage was now set for the

---

[23] Luke 5:1-11 NKJV

commissioning of the church. Jesus had received the attention of the people; now it was time to develop leaders who would later become leaders of the church to carry out the message to the uttermost parts of the earth. Jesus is preparing his band of disciples to preach the good news to the Jewish people, while at the same time providing the disciples with the necessary skills to plant churches among the Gentiles as the Jewish people reject them. "Luke's location of this story of the call of the first disciples implies that Jesus' popularity and the size of the crowds made it necessary to have helpers."[24] The text tells us that as Jesus is passing by the multitudes, the people pressed upon Him because of their hunger for the Word of God. "This scene is introduced by a reference to the crowds coming to see Jesus and closes with the report that the fisherman left everything to follow Jesus."[25]

Throughout his gospel, Luke portrays Jesus as a man with

---

[24] Fred B. Craddock, *Luke* (Louisville, KY: John Knox Press, 1990), 70.

[25] Leander E. Keck, *The New Interpreter's Bible*, vol. IX, *Luke, John* (Nashville, TN: Abingdon Press, 1995), 118.

a purpose who is strategic in fulfilling His kingdom assignment. This preceding encounter that Peter has with Jesus will change the course and direction of Peter's life, as well as have a lasting impact on those who would be looking on. Jesus senses the multitude following Him, and He maximizes the opportunity to be a master teacher, preacher, and recruiter. All of the aforementioned attributes are essential in church planting. At this point in His ministry, Jesus had acted alone in fulfilling His kingdom assignment described throughout the prophetic books of the Old Testament. Jesus begins the call to his future disciples on the Lake of Gennesaret. This is significant for the church planter because this is a turning point in the ministry of Jesus. According to Luke's gospel, "the last time we heard Jesus preach was in the synagogue; now he is at the lakeside." [26] Bill Easum writes, "the church planter needs to spend 50 percent of [their] time making contact with the

---

[26] William Barclay, *The Gospel of Luke* (Louisville, KY: Westminster John Knox Press, 2001), 67.

public."[27]

The Galilean Ministry of Jesus is all set to begin; as the Jewish people have rejected Him, and the Galileans gladly receive the liberating message of Christ, they are being prepared to further carry out the Gospel. As Jesus is preparing mentally to deliver the Word of God to the masses of people following Him, He notices two boats standing by, and apparently he knows the owner of the boats as well. Orion Hutchinson notes, "Since the Sea of Galilee was not far from Nazareth, the place where Jesus was raised, he probably visited there often and knew some of those who fished there for a living."[28] He asks Simon, the owner, to push out the boats a little from the land and into the sea. The specifics of Jesus' actions suggest He knew something and he was just waiting for the right moment. In the world of church planting, especially in the African-American context, timing is essential due to the culture

---

[27] Jim Griffith and Bill Easum, *Ten Most Common Mistakes Made by New Church Starts* (St. Louis, MO: Chalice Press, 2008), 52.

[28] Orion N. Hutchinson, Jr., *Basic Bible Commentary*, vol. 19, *Luke* (Nashville, TN: Abingdon Press, 1988), 134.

and communal aspects that are involved; for example, social trends such as housing projects, economic status, political make-up, various needs of the community, etc. Francis writes, "When a pastor feels the call to plant a church, he will do well to get wise counsel, develop support, organize a strong core group, and be fully appraised of the community before planting a new church."[29]

Jesus, being the prophet that He is, chooses the right time to speak to the crowds, while at the same time establishing organizational structure for the future of the church. During this time, leading priests and rabbis would have been seen gathering groups of students together in an effort to teach them the Torah. We will later learn that the gathering that Jesus hosted would have much greater value than the teaching of the Law—He was building networks and relationships for the purpose of fulfilling it.[30]

---

[29] Hozell C. Francis, *Church Planting in the African-American Context* (Grand Rapids, MI: Zondervan, 1999), 34.

[30] Francois Bovon, *A Commentary on the Gospel of Luke 1:1-9:50*, Hermeneia: A Critical & Historical Commentary on the Bible (Minneapolis, MN: Fortress Press, 2002), 169.

At this point in the gospel, Jesus symbolizes the Kingdom of God being fully present while at the same time not yet fully realized. This thought is significant in the Gospel of Luke due to the eschatological references made throughout his writings. This account of the call of the disciples serves as a point of reference for the activation of the process of eschatological fulfillment: "Now is a favorite word of Luke's: God's eschatological purposes are at this time being fulfilled in history."[31]

Peter's Redemptive Process

Competency

In Luke 4, Jesus is found healing Peter's mother-in law of a fever and restoring her back to wholeness. Reason would suggest that Jesus knew something about Peter and was strategic in his approach of evangelizing him. Throughout the gospels, Jesus and

---

[31] William Baird, "The Acts of Jesus in Galilee", *The Interpreter's One-Volume Commentary on the Bible*, ed. Charles M. Layman (Nashville, TN: Abingdon Press, 1971), 681.

Peter had several significant developmental encounters. These encounters were significant due to the importance of establishing identity. Peter would discover who Jesus is, and he would discover who he would become as a result of his relationship with Jesus.

In Matthew's gospel, Jesus and His disciples cross into the region of Caesarea Philippi, and He poses a question to them, "'Who do people say that the Son of Man is?' And they said, 'Some say John the Baptist, but others Elijah, and still others Jeremiah or one of the prophets.' He said to them, 'But who do you say that I am?' Simon Peter answered, 'You are the Messiah, the Son of the living God.'"[32] This moment between Jesus and Peter is one of self-discovery and affirmation in the life of Peter: "And Jesus answered him, 'Blessed are you, Simon son of Jonah! For flesh and blood has not revealed this to you, but my Father in heaven. And I tell you, you are Peter, and on this rock I will build my church, and the gates of Hades will not prevail against it.'"[33] Jesus establishes Peter's identity, calling him a "rock" and a foundation in

---

[32] Matthew 13:13-16 NRSV
[33] Matthew 13:17-18 NRSV

establishing the church. The words that Jesus uses "points to Peter as a leader among the apostles, who will play a foundational role in the early church."[34] Jesus finds the perfect time for the power of His message to transform the life of Peter.

Principles

Moreover, Jesus takes advantage of the opportunity to call Simon Peter to come and serve with Him in establishing the Kingdom of God on earth as it is in heaven. Luke writes, "When He (Jesus) had finished speaking, He said to Simon, 'Launch out into the deep water and let down your nets for a catch.'" Peter responds by saying, "Master we have worked all night long but have caught nothing, nevertheless if you say so, I will let down my nets for a catch."[35] In the redemptive work of Christ, Jesus is challenging the church at large to establish a new commitment to Himself. In humble submission, Peter listens to the anointed carpenter as He instructs him on being a fisherman. Throughout

---

[34] Arnold, *Zondervan Illustrated Bible Background Commentary*, 103.

[35] Luke 5:4-5 NRSV

the gospels, whenever Jesus is teaching, His teaching is followed by demonstrations of power or parables. I would like to imagine that just before this miracle, Jesus told the people on the lake a parable that Peter couldn't quite understand. Then He invites Peter to understand by experiencing what His teachings mean.

Character

This encounter finds Peter in the initial stages of comprehending the person and work of Christ. As a result of this interaction, Peter responds to the words and instruction of Christ and finds himself being overwhelmed by the results. The catch of the fish has not only impacted Peter, but also everyone else present. "This is the first miracle that was not a healing or an exorcism. Jesus does not command the sea or the fish, nor does he instruct the fisherman to do anything out of the ordinary."[36] As the miracle takes place, Peter immediately calls his partners to come and help him with the catch of the fish.[37] "The astounding catch of

---

[36] *The New Interpreter's Bible,* Volume IX, 118.

[37] Keener, Craig S. *The Bible Background Commentary* (Downers Grove, IL: InterVarsity Press, 1993), 201.

that morning astonished everyone present."[38] But how much more did this experience shape the life of Peter, who would later became one of the founding Apostles of the Church! "Simon is brought personally into the sphere of Jesus' mighty power and that experience becomes the basis of a promise made to him."[39] The promise Jesus made to Simon was the result of following His instructions. When the church planter is called to go into the harvest, they must follow Jesus' instructions and live with the anticipation of being fishers of men.

Transformation

During my undergraduate studies, I had a professor by the name of Dr. Christopher Hall who likened the call of Peter to the words of Dietrich Bonheoffer. Hall describes Peter's "Call to Discipleship" as a call to change, moving from self-denial to self-

---

[38] John Phillips, *Exploring the Gospel of Luke* (Grand Rapids, MI: Kregel Publications, 2005), 101.

[39] Joseph Fitzmyer, *The Gospel According to Luke I-IX*, vol. 28, *Anchor Bible* (New York, NY: Doubleday & Company, 1981), 562.

awareness. Internally Peter knew that something was going on but had no clue that Jesus was preparing him to be a disciple. After the catch was complete, through utter shame and embarrassment, Peter is recorded as declaring himself a sinful man: "Simon, conscious of his utter sinfulness and unworthiness to associate with such a person as Jesus, drops to his knees in reaction."[40] Jesus, who is mission-minded, never responds to Peter's declaration of himself but instead affirms him and gives him the details of his new job description: "Do not be afraid; from now on you will be catching people."[41] As church planters preparing to use a redemptive process and establish a redemptive work through the context of church planting, we must be confident in the fact that just as Jesus saw something in Peter, he sees something within us as He is preparing us as leaders to establish the Kingdom of God on earth as it is in heaven.

Fitzmyer suggests that, "Jesus' real message comes through

---

[40] Phillips, *Exploring the Gospel of Luke*, 101.
[41] Luke 5:10 NRSV

the 'bark of Peter.'"[42] The tension within the call develops intangibles needed to survive in the climate of church planting. At some point of the journey, one must develop a dependency on the power of the Triune God. In addition to the dependency that was being established, Luke's message empowers humanity with the accountability and responsibility of carrying out the commands of Jesus.

Redemptive

This commission finds Jesus at the initial stages of His public ministry, hand-picking His successors. He has the unique ability to take our strengths and weaknesses and use our personalities in the Kingdom as we see Him successfully doing with Peter and his fellow laborers: "The metaphor of the fisherman catching human beings for the Kingdom implies a role of agency, linked to the ministry of Jesus himself."[43] Peter and his fellow fisherman respond to the call by leaving everything behind and

---

[42] Fitzmyer, *The Gospel According to Luke I-XI*, 562.

[43] Fitzmeyer, *The Gospel According to Luke I-XI*, 569.

following Him. This text suggests that they left the big catch that they may obtain an even bigger catch for the Kingdom of God.

The summation of this verse speaks to the various models of church planting, due to the variations of worship styles within our churches. If this ideology was considered and discussed, the church would have a greater opportunity for unity and transparency across generational and denominational lines: "When they had brought their boats to shore, they left everything and followed Him."[44] "Thus the call of the disciples is given a dramatic setting; the mission of God is grounded in the miracle of divine action."[45] As a result, two thousand years later, there are over 2 billion Christians in the world—that was a catch worth risking it all. Church planting in the African-American context is a risk, church planting in any context is a risk; however, when men and women experience the redemptive power of Christ as a result of pastors being obedient to the words and the work of Christ, it's a process worth enduring.

---

[44] Luke 5:11 NRSV

[45] Baird, "The Acts of Jesus in Galilee", 681.

Summary

The mission of the church is expressed by the fulfillment of the Great Commission. "We are living in a generation of African Americans who are significantly unchurched. For three centuries, the black church stood as the central institution of black life. Its relevance was unquestioned and its moral and spiritual capital unparalleled."[46] According to Dr. Ellis,

Increasing numbers of African Americans are looking for theological answers. The church is strategically positioned to meet this challenge. While the traditional church has played a key role in the Black experience, it is not equipped for the task before us in its present state. It will continue to be unable to connect with those who are seeking answers to their theological questions. Addressing these concerns requires new models of the church – models able to appreciate the old traditions yet armed with theology that is biblical, cognitive and applied to addressing legitimate African American cultural core concerns.

This partly explains the increased efforts at church planting among African Americans, and the need for a return to a biblical

---

[46] Thabiti M. Anyabwile, *The Decline of African American Theology* (Downers Grove, IL: InterVarsity, 2007), 245.

understanding of addressing African American cultural core concerns.[47]

Through this report, Dr. Ellis provides us with a theological framework that establishes the significance and purpose of church planting in the African-American context. According to Major Jones, "the history of Black Theology was birthed out of the need to clearly establish our identity in relation to Christianity." Jones describes Black Theology as an expression of history as well as a present reality: "Black Theology in its historical perspective is meant to serve as the launching pad in our ongoing quest in fulfilling our responsibility in obtaining liberation for all people".[48]

In conclusion, Jesus, the Apostle Paul, and Peter had a great impact in establishing and redeeming the church through church planting due to their ability to study and embrace the

---

[47] *African-American Church Planting Research Report.*
[48] Major J. Jones, *The Color of God: The Concept of God in Afro-American Thought* (Macon, GA: Mercer University Press, 1990), 5.

culture. If we as church planters desire to be effective, we must become students of the culture, and allow our experience to help us contextualize an evangelistic strategy of greater relevancy.

The theological and biblical framework of this chapter leads us into our literature review. There are significant contributions to the work of church planting in the African-American Church. Hozell Francis balances the importance of establishing a strong theological presence in the framing and building of the church. In addition to Francis, Michael J. Cox and Joe Samuel Ratliff co-author a book entitled, *Church Planting in the African American Community*, where their focus is primarily on the practical attributes that church planters must embrace. In addition to their works, LifeWay Research has just recently completed a full report on African-American church planting. These references are the most directly related work on the subject. Ed Stetzer, author of *Planting Missional Churches*, makes significant contributions to the principles and strategies of church planting.

CHAPTER III

LITERATURE & KEY THEMES OF THE MODEL

The purpose of this chapter is to identify the significant sources that will contribute to the goal of establishing a Redemptive Model for Church Planting in the African-American context. The literature involved in this significant work has evolved over the last decade due to the rise of church planting in the African-American context. LifeWay Research "surveyed 290 African-American church planters who started churches prior to 2012… Church planters from more than 20 denominations participated plus several from non-denominational churches."[1] The study also

---

[1] Ed Stetzer, "African-American Church Planting," *Christianity Today*, September 4, 2013, accessed November 11, 2013, http://www.christianitytoday.com/edstetzer/2013/septemb

found a steady increase in attendance to be the overall trend among African-American church starts.

As a result of the growth of church planting in the African-American context, there has been a conscious demand for scholarship and statistical data that would assist church planters in their purpose and strategies, a process that would ultimately serve as a guiding compass for the future. Ed Stetzer, one of the leading authors on the subject of church planting, writes, "I would welcome more scholarship on this vital subject from church planting experts and authors who have personal experience to share."[2]

LifeWay research discovered, "This research has begun productive conversations among church planting leaders across the United

---

er/new-research-on-african-american-church-planting.html.

[2] Ed Stetzer, *Planting Missional Churches* (Nashville, TN; Boardman & Holman, 2006), 121.

States about how best to train and equip new church plants led by African-American planters in African-American contexts."[3]

As a result of those conversations, several books have been published and research has been conducted for the purpose of developing and strengthening those commissioned with church planting in the African-American community. Before the LifeWay Research report, the most direct published works on the subject were *Church Planting in the African-American Context* written by Hozell C. Francis and *Church Planting in the African-American Community* by Michael J. Cox and Joe Samuel Ratliff. These authors made significant contributions to the life of the Redemptive Model of Church Planting in the African-American context. Francis provides a thesis that is both practical and academic. His contributions to the model are of great significance due to his reinforcement of core values that are a necessity when entering the world of church planting. The values consist of shaping vision, planning wisely, knowing your community,

---

[3] Stetzer, "African-American Church Planting," *Christianity Today*, September 4, 2013.

leading effectively, reaching families, and transcending ethnic boundaries. All of these attributes are significant when attempting to establish a new perspective in a community within a community. "It is important that contemporary African-American church planters have an appreciation for the reasons that certain conditions exist within the context...an insensitivity to protocol can result in disaster."[4] Throughout his writings, Francis takes a collaborative approach among faith communities within the Body of Christ in order to reach the ultimate goal of effective ministry in the African-American context.

In addition to Francis, Michael J. Cox and Joe Samuel Ratliff also make a significant contribution to the Redemptive Model as their research flows out of the lenses of denominational leadership. They represent the Southern Baptist and American Baptist Church traditions respectively. Their foresight and vision throughout their research speaks directly to the pulse of the

---

[4] Hozell C. Francis, *Church Planting in the African-American Context* (Grand Rapids, MI: Zondervan, 1999), 64.

Redemptive Model. Ratliff and Cox conduct case studies on nine different church planting models in the Midwest region for the purpose of providing ten transforming lessons. These churches are unique to the model due to their denominational affiliations, and this brings a holistic view to the diversity presented within the model. The results of the case studies are presented as ten lessons:

1) The right church starter is a key to the success of a new church.
2) The new church must be creative and flexible when it comes to facilities.
3) Different methods reach different people.
4) The necessary resources include more than money.
5) The sponsoring church must take a businesslike approach.
6) The sponsoring church must have a vision for the kingdom of God.
7) The sponsoring church can sponsor more than one church at a time.
8) A new church must be accountable to its sponsoring church and vice versa.
9) The development of lay leadership should be a top priority for any new church.

10) The longer the tenure of the pastor, the greater the likelihood of success for the church.[5]

Cox and Ratliff demonstrate the reality of church planting whether from a denominational or independent perspective. "Setting goals that are realistic and achievable while seeking input to solutions from the sponsoring church and mentors will aid the planter in staying the course."[6]

In addition to the work by the aforementioned authors, Ed Stetzer's *Planting Missional Churches*, also makes a significant contribution to the model. Stetzer doesn't take a cultural approach; rather, his focus is primarily on the biblical principles, various models, and strategic applications that are based on experience and decades of research. Stetzer's work is of great significance as

---

[5] Michael J. Cox and Joe Samuel Ratliff, *Church Planting in the African-American Community* (Valley Forge, PA: Judson Press, 2002), 41.

[6] Cox and Ratliff, *Church Planting in the African-American Community*, 42.

the African-American community produces church planters in a diverse and global society.

LifeWay Research and the Lewis Center for Church Leadership have also conducted significant research on African-American Church Planting and New Church Development respectively. LifeWay Research's report was a cross-denominational project under the direction of Wy Plummer, Dr. Carl Ellis, Jr., and Ed Stetzer. The object of this study was to "quantitatively measure characteristics of African-American church plants and to identify characteristics that are related to higher attendance or higher numbers of new commitments to Jesus Christ, to measure the health of African-American church plants, and to measure characteristics that are distinctive to the African-American context."[7] The thesis of this report aligns

---

[7] LifeWay Research, "African-American Church Planting Research Report," last modified July 15, 2013, accessed November 10, 2013, http://pcamna.org/wordpress/wp-content/uploads/2013/08/African-American-Church-Planting-Final-Quantitative-Research-Report.pdf.

directly with the purpose and significance of the Redemptive Model.

The Lewis Center for Church Leadership's research centers focus on church planting as a vehicle of redemption. Their research asks pivotal questions as to the Why? Where? What? and How? in an effort to provide strategic insights to church planters. "The Lewis Center is building a new vision for church leadership grounded in faith, informed by knowledge, and exercised in effective practice."[8]

Furthermore, all of these works are significant to the contribution of the Redemptive Model as they all reinforce the necessity to stay the course, and they provide church planters the opportunity to garner as many tools as possible that we may be effective in the work of the Kingdom.

As a result of our research and case studies these themes have emerged as effective in equipping the church planter with the

---

[8] Lewis Center for Church Leadership, accessed December 11, 2013, www.churchleadership.com.

necessary tools to build a solid foundation in the establishment of a church and or organization.

Key Themes

Being Relational

Pastors, scholars, authors, and devoted disciples all agree that there is great significance in building and cultivating relationships. The relational aspect of ministry has a tremendous value and impact. Julia T. Wood writes, "Interpersonal communication is the foundation of our personal and professional identity and growth, and it is the primary basis of building connections with others." [9] George Barna and Harry Jackson write, "The person-to-person connections facilitated in churches becomes the fuel that propels…It all starts with a determination by church leaders to invite people into a genuine family in which love freely flows and is advanced by an environment in which each individual sees the benefits of connecting with others on the same

---

[9] Julia T. Wood, *Interpersonal Communication Everyday Encounters* (Belmont, CA: Wadsworth, 2002), 11.

journey of significance."[10] Throughout the New Testament, Jesus and Paul model the significance of building and cultivating relationships. For three and a half years Jesus builds relationships with His disciples and the surrounding community for the purpose of spreading the gospel. The Apostle Paul takes on the role of mentor and community builder as he mentors Timothy and Titus, and he establishes a working relationship with Barnabas and others for the purpose of advancing the mission of Christ. In addition to the models of Paul and Jesus, the Apostles, under the leadership of Peter, cultivate a culture of home Bible studies: "The cultivated home group is a Bible study of a different kind. The planter uses the home group to cultivate the unchurched person's relationship with Christ and to develop the new leader's maturity in Christ."[11]

---

[10] George Barna and Harry R. Jackson, *High Impact African-American Churches* (Ventura, CA: Regal Books, 2004), 190.

[11] Stetzer, *Planting Missional Churches*, 208.

Prayer and the Great Commission

In addition to relationship building, the spiritual discipline of prayer is a valuable asset in connecting leaders and new converts: "Prayer generally follows and grows out of worship...This time can bind group members and empower their growth."[12] Jim Griffith and Bill Easum write "In their zeal to pursue the Great Commission, they [i.e. church planters] ignore the One for whom they're planting the church – God."[13] Throughout the history of the church, prayer has been and will continue to be a foundational principle in the progress and growth of the church. In addition to prayer, the Great Commission has been an essential component in accomplishing the task of church planting:

And Jesus came and said to them, "All authority in heaven and on earth has been given to me. Go therefore and make disciples of all nations, baptizing them in the name of the Father and of the Son

---

[12] Stetzer, *Planting Missional Churches*, 210.

[13] Jim Griffith and Bill Easum, *Ten Most Common Mistakes Made by New Church Starts* (Danvers, MA, 2008), 5.

and of the Holy Spirit, and teaching them to obey everything that I have commanded you. And remember, I am with you always, to the end of the age."[14]

The words of Jesus are foundational instructions for evangelism and cross-cultural missions, as we are challenged and instructed to be active and direct in our witness for Christ[15] Francis writes, "An effective contextually relevant approach to outreach will enable the new church to focus primarily on new converts in order to achieve growth. The Great Commission will be fulfilled as well."[16]

Moreover, the Great Commission provides a significant biblical and theological framework to the person and work of Jesus Christ. Michael J. Cox and Joe Samuel Ratliff write, "The point of

---

[14] Matthew 28:18-20 NRSV

[15] Mary Fairchild, "What is the Great Commission?", accessed November 17, 2013, http://christianity.about.com/od/glossary/f/greatcommission.htm.

[16] Francis, *Church Planting in the African-American Context*, 31.

Jesus' necessary journey is clear: the gospel is for all people, in all the world."[17]

Strategic Planning

The art of strategic planning in the context of ministry is essential. Church planting is a unique ministry opportunity that has the potential to impact the lives of new converts in a practical and relevant way. The discipline of strategic planning enables the researcher to examine the culture and the context in pursuit of establishing a clear vision that will ultimately lead to a clarity of vision that will provide a strong foundation for the on going work of the church. Strategic Planning is commonly known as a business principle that has enormous value in the development and implementation of establishing a church or non-profit organization. Aubrey Malphurs, in *Advanced Strategic Planning: A New Model for Church and Ministry Leaders*, provides the Christian Church with a tool that is progressive and necessary in

---

[17] Cox and Ratliff, *Church Planting in the African-American Community*, 4.

constructing plans that will be effective for the ongoing work of ministry. Strategic Planning and preparation are in direct contrast to one another. Hozell Francis writes, "I soon discovered the importance of preparing for church planting, being prepared may suggest a number of things. One is to attend seminars and the other is to read everything that is being done in contemporary church planting."[18] Furthermore, at the conclusion of this project, our goal is to identify strategic planning principles that are strategic in providing a model for church planting in the African-American context. (See Appendix B)

Strategic Evangelism

Hozell Francis writes, "One must consider an effective outreach methodology prior to planting a church."[19] One of the core values of my home church was "Strategic Evangelism," a value

---

[18] Francis, *Church Planting in the African-American Context*, 27.

[19] Francis, *Church Planting in the African-American Context*, 30.

that invites the leading disciples to be creative in their approach to discipleship. Drs. Gardener Taylor and Samuel Proctor write in their book, *We Have This Ministry,* "Our culture is a given; we are all children and products of it, having said that, culture is not a prison."[20] Proctor and Taylor demonstrate for us that the necessity of having a broader worldview in order for us to be effective in spreading the gospel. The world has become more diverse and global, and as a result, people of all cultures and communities have been impacted. According to Dr. Ellis, "African-American culture today has greater diversity than at any time in its history...therefore cross-cultural contacts have become commonplace. Currently, most African-Americans clearly identify with their own culture, yet resist being confined by it."[21]

---

[20] Samuel D. Proctor and Gardner C. Taylor, *We Have This Ministry,* (Valley Forge, PA: Judson Press, 1996), 4.

[21] Ed Stetzer, "Observations and Implications of African American Church Planting," *Christianity Today,* July 25, 2013, accessed December 11, 2013, http://www.christianitytoday.com/edstetzer/2013/july/observations-and-implications-of-african-american-church-pl.html.

One of the most effective tools of ministry is evangelism. Evangelism, when properly executed by serving and showing compassion, will ultimately lead potential converts into a relationship with Jesus Christ: "Successful African-American church planters are aware of this phenomenon and a contemporary worship style is best suited to reaching the demographic of the target community."[22]

Community Relations

While attending Northern Baptist Theological Seminary, I had the privilege of serving as the Community Relations Representative, where I was charged with being the voice and face of the seminary. If there was an event in the community, the seminary's required presence was fulfilled by my presence or a phone call acknowledging the event. As a result, the community and the seminary had a healthy, growing relationship. Ed Stetzer

---

[22] Stetzer, "Observations and Implications of African American Church Planting," *Christianity Today*, July 25, 2013.

writes, "It is not necessary for the church as an institution to be the hub of the community for its presence to be felt. The scattered church approach enables the church planter to become pastor of the whole community."[23]

In our context of ministry, we were invited to participate in the community business association meetings, where all the business owners and government officials of the community gather. Opportunities such as these allow the reach of the church to be extended for the greater work of the ministry and its ultimate success: "The more time a church planter has for such sustained and focused creative ministry around the felt concerns of the community, the more likely the success of the new church."[24]

Francis notes,

The black church has played a comprehensive and multifaceted role in its community. Primarily this has been necessary because

---

[23] Stetzer, "Observations and Implications of African American Church Planting," *Christianity Today*, July 25, 2013.

[24] Stetzer, "Observations and Implications of African American Church Planting," *Christianity Today*, July 25, 2013.

many avenues for social, economic, and political expressions were closed to African-Americans. The future of the development of society in politics and economics will determine how important the church's traditional role will continue to be.[25]

Leadership Development

Tom Nebel and Gary Rohrmayer, authors of *Church Planting Landmines*, write, "Every new church needs a leadership culture…no longer will you pray for God to bring you leaders, because leadership development will become normal and effective in your new church."[26] As the Redemptive Model evolves within the church planting community, leadership development will be a significant attribute; however, leadership development takes time and discernment: "African American church planters should be encouraged to participate in church planting boot camps, as they

---

[25] Francis, *Church Planting in the African-American Context*, 76.

[26] Tom Nebel and Gary Rohrmayer, *Church Planting Landmines* (St. Charles, IL: ChurchSmart Resources, 2005), 30.

promote valuable basic principles that apply universally."[27] Traditionally, the African-American approach to leadership was considered to be the pastor as the "lone wolf"; however, the Redemptive Model encourages a team leadership approach directed and supervised alongside the pastor: "A team leadership approach to church planting would probably be more effective than the lone wolf approach."[28] Drs. Rodney L. Cooper and Claude R. Alexander write, "a well defined understanding of team and organizational development based on a solid knowledge of theological, development, and sociological principles pertaining to redemptive leadership in a team and organizational context will hopefully result in hope, encouragement and renewal of vision in regard to developing healthy teams and organizations."[29]

---

[27] Stetzer, "Observations and Implications of African American Church Planting," *Christianity Today*, July 25, 2013.

[28] Stetzer, "Observations and Implications of African American Church Planting," *Christianity Today*, July 25, 2013.

[29] Drs. Claude R. Alexander and Rodney L. Cooper, "African-American Redemptive Leadership: Foundations

Stewardship

The finances of the church are always considered to be a sensitive topic. However, the redemptive model stresses the importance of teaching biblical principles of stewardship that will allow people to mature in their approach to giving: "We must begin to earnestly teach our people the biblical principles of stewardship. This can be done in seminars, sermons, literature, and most importantly in practice."[30] Jim Griffith and Bill Easum write, "Discipleship is a heart issue; virtue capital is a money issue, every church plant should take an offering from the very beginning."[31] Francis adds, "People must be taught that giving is indeed an integral part of worship and that God's people are not to be begging. Beyond teaching people to give their tithes and

---

and Development of Teams" (lecture, Gordon-Conwell Theological Seminary, Charlotte, NC, September 21, 2012).

[30] Francis, *Church Planting in the African-American Context*, 83.

[31] Jim Griffith and Bill Easum, *Ten Most Common Mistakes Among Church Planters* (St. Louis, MO: Chalice Press, 2008), 86.

offerings on a consistent basis, urban church leaders must teach their members the benefit of pooling their resources."[32] (See Appendix C)

Summary

A Redemptive Model for church planting in the African-American context primarily serves as a model of transition as the historical church meets the contemporary church head on: "As the pace of civil rights gains began to accelerate, African-Americans began to move into previously uncharted waters, and they began to encounter issues beyond the traditional scope."[33] As a result, our freedoms stretched the African-American community, culture, and content, which ultimately sent the church searching for a new identity: "The church continued to be the strongest institution in the African-American community, but the quality of its influence went from primarily theological in 1900, then to sociological by

---

[32] Francis, *Church Planting in the African-American Context*, 84.

[33] "African-American Church Planting Research Report."

the 1960's. Today, its influence is primarily stylistic."[34] Statements such as these, cry out for the necessity of a Redemptive Model in the African-American church and community for the purpose of presenting and implanting creative ministry concepts: "The shifting dynamics of the target community necessitate the formation of new creative ministries, to overcome this, the church plant should maintain a strong emphasis on creative ministries, and flexibility in developing new ones."[35]

The need for this model is illustrated by Jesus' statement in the gospels, "new wine needs to be put in new wineskins."[36] Rodney L. Cooper writes, "New wine needs to be in flexible skins so the skin has room to expand as it ferments. If it is put into the old, brittle skin, it will burst the skin. Jesus was making the point the new order and the old order are incompatible."[37] Therefore,

---

[34] "African-American Church Planting Research Report."
[35] "African-American Church Planting Research Report."
[36] Mark 2:22 NKJV
[37] Rodney L. Cooper, *Mark*, Holman New Testament Commentary (Nashville, TN: Broadman & Holman Reference, 2000), 35.

Jesus challenges the New Testament Church and validates the purpose and intention of the Redemptive Model. The call is to establish a new perspective on a significant work that has unlimited value and potential:

Those who wish to reach African-Americans must create ministries beyond the parameters and limitations of the traditional African-American and non -American church. If this can be accomplished, these church plants may reach many cultures and generations, even those who are hostile to Christianity. This is especially true given the global appeal of contemporary African-American culture.[38]

In conclusion, as we transition into Chapter IV, the literature review provides the researcher with key themes that give reason and purpose for presenting a redemptive model of church planting in the African-American context. The framework of the redemptive model—consisting of competency, principles, character, transformation, and redemption—provides an avenue for the key ideals and themes to emerge from our readings: the significance of being relational, prayer, the Great Commission,

---

[38] "African-American Church Planting Research Report."

strategic planning and evangelism, the necessity for leadership development, and the importance of stewardship. In addition to the key ideals and themes, Stetzer outlines three biblical models of church planting that are key in establishing a Redemptive Model for the African-American church. The trends presented in these models transition the researcher into the chapter on methodology, where our goal is to present several models that will benefit the ongoing process of the redemptive work in the African-American church. Stetzer points out that "many different biblical models are effective in planting a church, and God does not bless one way more than the others."[39] As a result, we are presented with a redemptive model and framework that serves as a guideline for the exposition and project design in Chapter IV.

---

[39] Stetzer, *Planting Missional Churches*, 53.

CHAPTER IV

THE DESIGN OF THE MODEL

Introduction

The primary purpose of this chapter is to explore the hypotheses. The question behind the research will be answered by providing a description of the project's function: to fulfill the need for presenting a redemptive leadership model for church planters in the African-American context of ministry (chapter I). Chapter II provides us the theological and biblical framework, while chapter III provides a literature review that outlines principles for church planting: being relational, prayer, commissioning, strategic planning, evangelism, community relations, leadership development, and stewardship. These principles will be incorporated into a study of three unique models of church plants in the African-American context.

Stetzer's chapter, "Models of Church Plants and Church planters," speaks to the structure and framework of the Redemptive Model. In this chapter three models of church planting are presented: "The most common patterns or models explained in this chapter are based on research, observation, and conversation with church planters."[1]

---

[1] Ed Stetzer, *Planting Missional Churches* (Nashville, TN: Boardman & Holman, 2006), 53.

Model	The Apostolic Harvest Church Planter[2]	The Founding Pastor[3]	Team Planting[4]
Paradigm	<ul><li>starts church</li><li>raises up leaders from the harvest</li><li>moves to start new church</li></ul>	<ul><li>starts a church</li><li>acts as a "church planter" for a short time</li><li>remains long term to pastor the new church</li></ul>	<ul><li>a group of planters relocates into an area to start a church</li><li>often the team has a senior pastor.</li></ul>
Biblical Model	<ul><li>Paul</li></ul>	<ul><li>Peter</li></ul>	<ul><li>Paul (at times)</li></ul>
Historic/Modern Examples	<ul><li>Methodist circuit riders</li><li>house church movement</li><li>network of house churches</li></ul>	<ul><li>Charles Spurgeon</li><li>Rick Warren</li></ul>	<ul><li>missionaries at Iona</li><li>team church plants</li></ul>
Principles	<ul><li>Planter starts church and moves on.</li><li>Pastor comes out of the church and then goes back into it.</li><li>Pastor may or may not be classically educated.</li><li>New churches provide core for additional congregations.</li></ul>	<ul><li>Planter starts and pastors the church long term.</li><li>Pastor often moves from another location.</li><li>Pastor often classically educated.</li><li>Ideally, new church sponsors new congregations.</li></ul>	<ul><li>A team relocates to plant a new church.</li><li>Church planting vision often comes from one key member of the team.</li><li>Good teams have a gift mix.</li><li>Team may amicably split up from the mother church into multiple daughter churches or become traditional staff members of the founded church.</li></ul>

[2] Stetzer, *Planting Missional Churches*, 54.
[3] Stetzer, *Planting Missional Churches*, 61.
[4] Stetzer, *Planting Missional Churches*, 71.

As a result, each model of church planting presents its own unique dynamics, which are based on biblical, historical and cultural principles. The researcher's goal in this project is to present a model that is specific to the African-American context of ministry; however, as Stetzer points out, "The call of God and his provision of spiritual gifts will determine how each church planter accomplishes the work of starting new churches."[5]

Process Overview

The problem this research seeks to address is to examine the significant factors that can serve as a redemptive model for African-American church planters. To make this determination, it is of great necessity to select a research method that will aid the researcher in addressing the problem. For this project, we have chosen the case study research method. We selected three pastors and churches in the state of Maryland who have planted churches in the African-American community.

---

[5] Stetzer, *Planting Missional Churches*, 75.

Case Study Method

The case study method represents a type of research that is qualitative. "The case study method calls for discussion of real-life situations that business executives have faced."[6] Hammond also writes, "Case studies cut across a range of organizations and situations, they provide you with an exposure far greater than you are likely to experience in your day-to-day routine. They also permit you to build knowledge in various management subjects by dealing selectively and intensively with problems in each field."[7]

Robert K. Yin, author of *Case Study Research*, provides us with a technical definition of a case study: "A case study is an empirical inquiry that investigates a contemporary phenomenon

---

[6] John S. Hammond, "Learning by the Case Method," *Harvard Business School*, April 16, 2002, accessed December 14, 2013, http://sphweb.bumc.bu.edu/otlt/teachingLibrary/Case20Teaching/learning-by-case-method.pdf
[7] Hammond, "Learning by the Case Method," *Harvard Business School*, April 16, 2002.

within its real-life context, especially when the boundaries between phenomenon and context are not clearly evident."[8]

In the case of this research, the goal is to determine what selected church planters in the African-American community identified as key factors in establishing a redemptive model in the African-American church. The expected outcome is that this project will provide us with a methodology to assist church planters, pastors, and denominations in revitalizing their context of ministry by supporting and endorsing the work of church planting in the African-American community. Once our methodology has been established, our goal is to identify the method that will guide us in the process of addressing our research question. As a result, the case study method has been chosen because it is a tactical research tool that affords the researcher the opportunity for data collection in a unique format that wouldn't be available through quantitative analysis.

---

[8] Robert K. Yin, *Case Study Research: Design and Methods* (Thousand Oaks, CA: Sage Publications, 2003), 13.

Furthermore, the case study method allows the researcher to be more present as they are able to hear, read, and understand the nature and source of the personal convictions that has directed them in church planting in the African-American context. Hammond writes, "The case study method is a really focused form of learning by doing."[9]

Research and Hypothesis

The research for this project is designed to lead toward intentionally formulating a process that will illuminate the principles of church planting. Church planting is a redemptive work that has the ability to impact and influence cultures and communities. The question before us is, Can church planting using the redemptive model be an effective model within the African-American Church? There are several questions that we will ask that will aid us in drawing our conclusion. In addition to the questions we have conducted several case studies among African-American church planters. Robert Yin, author of *Case*

---

[9] Hammond, "Learning by the Case Method," *Harvard Business School*, April 16, 2002.

Study Research writes, "case studies are the preferred strategy when 'how' or 'why' questions are being posed, when the investigator has little control over the event, and when the focus is on a contemporary phenomenon within some real-life context."[10] In addition to the case studies, ten pastors who have planted churches and ten pastors of established churches participated in interviews and completed questionnaires. The essence of this research goes beyond quantitative data. However, our goal is to present the results from the qualitative interviews that would produce an African-American church planting qualitative report.

As a result, criteria was established for selected pastors and pastoral interviews were conducted within three stages, identify the personal vision of church planting, identify the implantation of the vision, and finally identify the results and experiences of the vision.

---

[10] Robert Yin, *Case Study Research: Design and Methods* (Thousand Oaks, CA: Sage Publications, 2003), 1.

Questionnaire for Pastors

The following questions were asked during each of the pastorals interviews.

Criteria 1: Church planting pastors in the African-American context were selected to identify their personal vision of church planting.

1) What experiences have led you to church planting in the African-American context?
2) In your estimation, what is the current state of the African-American church?
3) When you hear the word "redemption" in relation to the African-American church, what are your thoughts?
4) How does the African-American church connect with younger generations and the surrounding cultures and communities?
5) In your estimation, how is church planting viewed among established African-American pastors?
6) What's your vision for a redemptive model in the African-American context?

Criteria 2: Church planting pastors in the African-American context were selected to identify the implementation of the vision of church planting in the African-American context.

1) How is your church implanting a vision of the Redemptive Model?

2) How would the Redemptive Model of church planting in the African-American context, benefit the African-American church and community?
3) What's your theological rationale for church planting in the African-American context?
4) How can the traditional African-American church and the Redemptive Model of church planting complement one another?
5) In your estimation, what's the future of the African-American church?

Criteria 3: Church planting pastors in the African-American context were selected to share their results and experience of church planting in the African-American context.

1) How has your church progressed as a church plant in the African-American context?
2) What are the significant benchmarks that you would identify in the success and stability of the church?
3) What's the external perception of the church among the surrounding communities?
4) What if anything would you do differently as a church planter?
5) As a result of your experience, what would you identify as key themes in church planting in the African-American context?

Case Study 1: Gary Johnson, Sr., Faith Christian Worship Center

Competency

Reverend Gary G. Johnson, Sr., Emma Duncan and Naomi Lyde planted Faith Christian Worship Center. Rev. Johnson first openly shared the vision with Ms. Duncan and Ms. Lyde that God had inspired and given him a vision to plant a church in the African-American community. As a result, after a time of prayer and strategic planning, he planted Faith Christian Worship Center in 1996, a time when planting churches outside a denominational structure was considered rebellious and met with many contentions within the African-American community.

Pastor Johnson had great respect and admiration for the denominational structure, since he was reared in the African-Methodist Episcopal Zion Church. However, he felt that his gifts and calling that God had equipped him for was better suited for church planting. He is an avid reader and the writings of Dr. Tony Evans and John Piper began to shape his framework of ministry.

As a result, his journey in church planting in the African-American community had begun. One of the initial steps of the church plant was to clarify its identity. Pastor Johnson named the church Faith Christian Worship Center as a reflection of God's working in his life. Establishing the foundational principles of the church—principles built on faith, the Word of God and Evangelism—followed the naming of the church.

Principles

With the identity and the principles being established it was now time to be obedient to the call of God and prepare for the launch of the church. Pastor Johnson and his leaders partnered with an inner-city elementary school on the Westside of Baltimore. The partnership led to the school allowing the church to use the space for Sunday Morning Worship. After three months of planning and evangelizing, Faith Christian Worship Center launched its first worship service in the auditorium of the school with 150 people in attendance. The first four months of the ministry began in partnership with the Harlem Park Elementary/Middle School.

After much time, the strategic planning team came up with a plan to partner up with another inner-city school in an effort to establish the foundational principles of evangelism within the workings of the church; therefore, a new partnership was established with Rosemont Elementary School. The church partnered for three years with the school, giving them full access to the facilities, and the church leaders were vibrant partners in the school and surrounding community.

Character

With the ministry being established within the community, the focus shifted to organizational structure. The church was able to lease a church building not far from the schools in which they served. For six years, the church was able to establish the structure and body of the church through their evangelistic efforts, which placed the church in a position to purchase their own worship space. Over a ten-year span, serving four communities, the church found itself purchasing their own building with full-service options for their congregation and the needs of the community. The building that they purchased was in a 5-mile radius of all the communities, which they were able to evangelize.

Transformation

The demographics of the community is predominantly African-Americans living in low-income housing. The median household income is significantly below the state average with the unemployment percentage above the state average. There's a wide range of ages within the community, many 2nd generation renters, living together in an effort to balance expenses. Faith Christian Worship Center has become very aware of the needs of the community in relation to job creation, home ownership, education, and financial empowerment. The stakeholders within the ministry have made their resources available and partnered with the surrounding business community in an effort to bring resources and hope to the community. The stakeholders of Faith

Christian Worship Center are Deacons and Community Leaders who have grown their businesses and influence alongside the development of the church. As a result of their salvation and maturity in Christ, they have been intentional in being invested in the growth of the church and surrounding communities. One of the stakeholders is the Vice-President of the National Fraternity, Phi Beta Sigma Fraternity Incorporated, and owner of the Rodent and Commercial Cleaning Service. The ages of the members of the church are between 25-45. Many of them are first generation Christians who are active in the discipleship process.

Redemption

As a result, Faith Christian Worship Center is focused on fulfilling the Great Commission by providing an atmosphere of diligence, commitment, and consistency through:

1. Bible Study (2 Timothy 2:15)
2. Prayer (Philippians 4:6)
3. Evangelism (Matthew 28:19)
4. Living Holy Daily (Romans 12:1—2)

5. God's Presence With Us (Matthew 28:20; Philippians 4:13)

Furthermore, Faith Christian Worship Center embodies their view redemption as a result of the vision:

To create an atmosphere where all men can be saved, nurtured, developed, educated, and empowered through Jesus Christ, economically, mentally, spiritually, physically, and socially. By doing this the children will be RECLAIMED, the sinners will be REDEEMED, and the broken hearted will be RESTORED to complete wholeness through the RECEIVING of Jesus Christ as Lord and Savior. By accomplishing this, we will meet the needs of the total man.[11]

Pastoral Interview

On October 5, 2013 I had the privilege of interviewing Pastor Gary Johnson at his office in Baltimore, Maryland. The

---

[11] Gary Johnson, "Welcome to the Website of Faith Christian Worship Center," Faith Christian Worship Center, accessed October 14, 2013, www.fcwc1.org.

interview lasted about an hour and a half. Pastor Johnson informed me that he has an undergraduate degree and is currently a graduate student. However, much of his education came as a result of reading as many books as possible on leadership, church growth, and strategic planning. The personal interview allowed me to hear his passion and excitement to serve the people of God. When I arrived at his church, his staff treated me with excellence and I was humbled by their hospitality. Pastor Johnson and a key staff member guided me on a tour of their facility and educated me on the history of the church plant as well as the future plans for the church. Pastor Johnson was humbled by the interview and answered every question with clear focus. His emphasis was on servant leadership. At the time of the interview, the church had just celebrated 17 years of ministry. Pastor Johnson said that at the 17th year, he feels the church members are just getting into the rhythm of the overall vision for the church and community. He stated that the development of leadership takes time. He is a focused leader, and he continues on the journey of church planting in the African-American context.

Case Study 2: Pastor Shawn Bell, Greater Paradise Christian Center

Competency

Greater Paradise Christian Center is a church plant in the African-American community of Baltimore, Maryland. Greater Paradise was birthed in 2003 under the leadership of Pastor Shawn Bell. He and seventy-five disciples were involved in the process of planting the church. Pastor Bell is a unique church planter because he has served several Methodist congregations before sensing a call of the Holy Spirit to establish a church outside of the denomination. As a result, Pastor Bell yielded to the call, and the people gathered in September 2003 for their first Sunday morning worship service. The motivation that brought about the birthing of Greater Paradise came as a result of a desire for redemption. Pastor Bell felt that the denominational structure was stagnant and ministry became about maintaining the status quo and following the book of discipline rather than the Word of God.

Principles

Moreover, he expressed the need to break out of the traditional model. He defines traditional "as the method of doing the same thing, the same way, bound to a system which is enforced by the political structure."[12] However, he acknowledges that there is great value in the denominational structure for those who are called to that method of ministry. Pastor Bell's foundational concept of ministry came within the structure of the denomination; however, he exposed himself to other fellowships and denominations. As a result of his exposure, he believes the Holy Spirit birthed something within him that increased his vision and capacity for ministry. Thus the framework for Greater Paradise was established.

The vision and mission of the church "is to reach a hungry world with the life giving message of salvation through Jesus Christ." The mission and vision is accomplished through the core values of:

---

[12] Pastor Shawn Bell, interview by author, Baltimore. September 14, 2013.

1. Discipleship
2. Evangelism
3. Fellowship
4. Ministry
5. Worship

Character

As a result of this framework, Pastor Bell has become a visionary leader who inspires the congregation and community with vision. Vision is essential to the person of Pastor Bell. He has unapologetic passion for evangelism as he has conducted workshops and seminars on marketing strategies and vision casting for the purpose of strengthen the work of the church and fulfilling the Great Commission.

Transformation

The church is located in the inner city of Baltimore, where crime and poverty are prevalent within a three-mile radius of the church. However, the church is centered in a senior community where there is, according to Pastor Bell, 75% home ownership. The demographics of the community do not represent the social status or ages of the members within the congregation. Many commute to Greater Paradise as a result of the calling and assignment to the church. The dominant age group of Greater Paradise is between 35-50. This group also makes up the demographic of major stakeholders in the church. Pastor Bell defines the major stakeholders, as having the ability to bring ideas and solutions to the table, practice the discipline of tithing, and be present and accounted for worship service and ministry meetings. He expressed that these attributes are essential in the development and progression of the church.

Redemption

Greater Paradise's model, serving and being exposed to the needs of their congregation and the surrounding communities, has shaped their view of redemption. In addition to their service, redemption has also shaped the culture of the church. One year prior to my study of the church, the church was faced with the tragedy of arson. Following a day of service, the church hosted a block party for the community, serving over 500 people with food, health screenings, and empowering opportunities for personal enhancement. Twelve hours following the event, the church was set on fire and burned to the ground. For the next twelve months, the church worshipped in the neighboring elementary school where they were determined to embody redemption as an example of the person and work of Jesus Christ. After the twelve-month period was over, the church was rebuilt and has become an example to the community of what redemption can do in the life of a believer of Jesus Christ.

Pastoral Interview

During my interview with Pastor Shawn Bell, he was very humbled and expressed his passion for church planting in the African-American community. Throughout our time he shared his vision, which is centered on redemption. He has a desire for the church to be a city within a city, as the church has a full-service beauty salon that serves the entire community including seniors and single mothers. In addition, he expressed a desire for a café that will serve breakfast and lunch and provide jobs for those within the church and community. During our time, Pastor Bell's visionary emphasis is the tool he uses to empower and encourage families to dream and prepare them with the necessary tools to compete in this global society. Greater Paradise also partners with the neighboring elementary schools for the purpose of building relationships among the families and the congregation. According to Pastor Bell, his personal highlight of the ministry is their annual thanksgiving dinner where they have worship service for an hour and immediately following their service, serve the entire community a full Thanksgiving dinner.

As a result of my time with Pastor Bell, I learned the significance of vision in church planting and how it empowers the African-American community. Greater Paradise has grown to over 400 disciples within a period of eleven years with a ministry focus on salvation, discipleship, community development and economic empowerment that brings life and hope to the city of Baltimore, providing a model of ministry for the African-American community. In addition to sharing with us the model of ministry for Greater Paradise, Pastor Bell constructed a thirty-minute workshop on strategic marketing for the purpose of evangelism and empowerment.

Case Study 3: Adams Chapel African Methodist Episcopal Church, Dr. Michael O. Thomas, Founder

Competency

Adams Chapel A.M.E. Church is unique to the Redemptive Model due to the fact that the church was planted out of a denominational setting. The rationale for the planting of the church came as a result of the denomination's desire to extend its presence throughout the city of Baltimore. Ed Stetzer labels this model, "The Apostolic Harvest Church Planter, where the planter starts the church, raises up leaders and moves to a new church."[13] This model serves as a more traditional model of church planting in the African-American context of ministry. However the church is called to be intentional in shaping a context and culture that

---

[13] Stetzer, *Planting Missional Churches*, 53.

meets the needs of the community in which they are called to serve. The church's website provides a more in depth rationale of the process of planting Adams Chapel:

> Adams Chapel African Methodist Episcopal Church was born out of the desire of the Baltimore Annual Conference presided over by Bishop John Hurst Adams, to expand the A.M.E. Church in the Conference boundaries. Adams Chapel was established as a mission church on Palm Sunday, April 4, 1982 and it was the first new A.M.E. church in Baltimore in 32 years. Adams Chapel A.M.E. Church was also the vision of the young Rev. Michael O. Thomas, a Deacon at Bethel A.M.E. in Baltimore, to establish a mission in the Liberty Heights community. Along with Rev. Michael Thomas and his wife, Rev. Debyii Thomas, came one hundred charter members. The members were former parishioners of Bethel A.M.E. in Baltimore, then under the Pastorship of Rev. Dr. John R. Bryant, who can be credited for spearheading this major effort of the Church. Because Rev. Thomas would not be ordained an Itinerant Elder until the next Annual Conference, the first communions were consecrated and

served to the new congregation by Rev. Mary Henry Whitehead of Bethel A.M.E. Church, Rev. Edward C. Wilson, Presiding Elder of the Eastern District, and Bishop Harrison James Bryant.[14]

Principles

The denominational structure provides the overall mission and vision of the church:

The Mission of the African Methodist Episcopal Church is to minister to the spiritual, intellectual, physical, emotional, and environmental needs of all people by spreading Christ's liberating gospel through word and deed. At every level of the Connection and in every local church, the African Methodist Episcopal Church shall engage in carrying out the spirit of the original Free African Society, out of which the AME Church evolved: that is, to seek out and save the lost, and serve the needy.[15]

---

[14] Adams Chapel AME Church, accessed December 11, 2013, www.adamschapelamechurch.org.

[15] African-Methodist Episcopal Church, accessed December 11, 2013, www.ame-church.com.

Character

The framework in fulfilling the mission of the church is based on six core values of the denomination:

1. Christian Discipleship
2. Christian Leadership
3. Current Teaching Methods & Materials
4. History & Significance of the AME Church
5. God's Biblical Principles
6. Social Development to which all should be applied to daily living.[16]

Transformation

The demographics of the church are an African-American population and unemployment rate that are above the state average, and a median household income that is below the state average. The primary intent of the church was to be placed in a community where the church can serve and empower the people. The major stakeholders welcome this opportunity to serve. In this

---

[16] African-Methodist Episcopal Church, accessed December 11, 2013, www.ame-church.com.

context the major stakeholders are the denomination, the mother church, and those one hundred people who were a part of the initial launch. The ages of the member range between 40-50. As a result, their view of redemption comes as result of their experience with the mother church and the long-standing influence and impact of the denomination. The mother church upon this planting was able to transform a community surrounded by poverty—a transformation that provides hope and a framework for the mission of the church to be fulfilled within this community.

Redemption

The redemptive process of Adams Chapel serves a model for the expansion of ministry within the denominational structure. Adams Chapel has been a beckon of light of the gospel of Jesus Christ for over thirty-two years. As a result many souls have been saved, communities and cultures have been impacted as a model of redemption has been proven and established.

Pastoral Interview

I had the privilege of interviewing the founder of Adams Chapel A.M.E Church, Dr. Michael O. Thomas, on May 7, 2013. This was a very educational and informative interview as he provided structure and detail to a church that was intentional and systematic. At the time of the church plant, Dr. Thomas was a young minister at the mother church of the conference Bethel A.M.E Church, which happened to be the largest and most influential church in the city. For two years leading up to the plant, Dr. Thomas lead a prayer group at 12 noon in the sanctuary of the mother church. In addition to the noonday prayer, the pastor had appointed five people to pray over the plant every Friday for an extended period. As a result of prayer, 100 disciples of the mother church agreed to join the young minister. In the process of launching the church, there was a strong investment in media and public relations. The mother church purchased newspaper ads and air time on television and radio for evangelistic commercials. In addition to evangelism, Thomas has a strong theological and biblical framework, as he speaks to the character and development of the black preacher who would be responsible for leading the church plant. Thomas references a book written by H. Beecher Hicks entitled, *The Image of the Black Preacher*. Dr. Thomas expressed throughout the interview that this was such a unique experience for the African-American community and moreover the African-American church. According to Stetzer, the model in which Thomas has founded is a model commonly identified with the African-American community: "This paradigm can be seen in the rapid growth of the Methodist and Baptist denominations in nineteenth-century America."[17]

Summary

These churches were selected because of their express interest in studying their church, community, and culture in an effort to be effective in their context. The pastors of these churches each saw this project as a larger part of their initiative to become strategic in reaching the African-American community. They

---

[17] Stetzer, *Planting Missional Churches*, 55.

113

acknowledged that in order to achieve the transformation desired, the right groups of committed people are essential. In addition to the people, the leadership and community must buy-in to the vision and strategies needed to have relevant ministry that impacts the generations of today as well as for the future.

Furthermore, the models of churches presented in this chapter present different methods in accomplishing their goals of effective ministry. However, within each of the models the key ideals and themes that emerged from our literature review in chapter 3 were demonstrated and a significant part of each model. As a result, the interviews with the respective pastors provided a summary of feedback to validate the researcher's findings, which will be described and outlined in chapter five.

CHAPTER V

THE PRESENTATION OF THE MODEL

Introduction

This chapter will present the results of the three unique church planting models as they apply to the problem. The case studies will be reviewed and a summary of the findings described. The findings will be discussed and the chapter will conclude with suggestions for further studies that are relevant to church planting in the African-American context. The case study method was used to provide a different perspective on three different models of church planting in the African-American context. These case studies demonstrate the significance of diversity of thought, strategic planning, and the power of vision. In addition, the case studies reveal the impact that context and culture can have within the faith community.

Summary of Results

While the three churches represented in the following case studies have many similarities, they also have some stark contrasts. The similarities include: inner-city church plants within a predominately African-American neighborhood, Methodist affiliation, minimum ten year existence, and a redemptive focus. Their redemptive focus is exhibited by their love for God and the person and work of Jesus Christ, their desire to fulfill the commands of Jesus through the Great Commission, and the strategic plan and process that are in place for the transforming partnership of culture, church, and community. Moreover the ministry exhibited by these churches demonstrate the contents of the redemptive model. Contents such as the competency of the call, fundamental principles, strength of character, transformation of communities and the power of redemption.

The case studies and questions reveal that the three churches represented serve different faith communities and have different philosophies of ministry; however, they all share the same goal and desire to impact their communities and empower their people through the gospel of Jesus Christ. The demographics of each church were similar and significant. All of the churches were planted in inner-city communities where the African-American population and the unemployment rates are above the state average; and the median household income, homeownership, and college graduates are below the state averages. According to the demographics, each church and community is planted in a prime area for those to benefit from a redemption model of ministry. Each church has a message of salvation for sinners, but their redemptive model focuses on using their brokenness as a way to further develop their relationship with Christ. Moreover, all three of these churches represent hope, restoration, and courage for the communities in which they are privileged to serve. Each church acknowledged their intent to be in the inner city amongst the people. Their preference of location was a desire to be a symbol of fulfillment and hope by meeting the needs of the communities at large.

Each pastor had a connection with the African Methodist Episcopal Church (AMEC). Dr. Michael Thomas has served the

AMEC for thirty-two years and represents the only active Methodist. Both Pastors Gary Johnson and Shawn Bell were reared and have served in the African Methodist Episcopal Zion Church for several years. This is significant due to the history of African-American Methodists:

The first separate denominations to be formed by African-Americans in the United States were Methodist. The early black Methodist churches, conferences, and denominations were organized by free black people in the North in response to stultifying and demeaning conditions attending membership in the white-controlled Methodist Episcopal churches. This independent church movement of black Christians was the first effective stride toward freedom by African-Americans.[1]

Furthermore, the mission and purpose of the AMEC has a redemptive focus:

---

[1] C. Eric Lincoln and Lawrence H. Mamiya. *The Black Church in the African American Experience* (Durham, NC: Duke University Press, 1990), 47.

Each local church of the African Methodist Episcopal Church shall be engaged in carrying out the spirit of the original Free African Society out of which the A.M.E. Church evolved, that is, to seek out and save the lost and serve the needy through a continuing program of: preaching the gospel, feeding the hungry, clothing the naked, housing the homeless, cheering the fallen, providing jobs for the jobless, administering to the needs of those in prisons, hospitals, nursing homes, asylums and mental institutions, senior citizens' homes, caring for the sick, the shut-in, the mentally and socially disturbed, and encouraging thrift and economic advancement.[2]

As a result of each pastor's exposure and education in the AMEC, their redemptive focus has an emphasis on service and awareness of social sensitivities within the church and surrounding communities.

---

[2] Lincoln and Mamiya, *The Black Church in the African American Experience*, 55.

Each church has been an established and effective presence in the area of church planting in the African-American community for over a decade. Their consistency has provided a sense of stability and demonstrated a culture of patience that is required for a newly organized church. The desire of the church plant is to cultivate relationships within and outside the communities they serve. All three of the pastors expressed how significant stability and endurance are to the implementation of effective strategies in pursuit of fulfilling the vision and mission of the church and community. Furthermore, the process of stability and endurance serves as the catalyst for achieving the primary goal of establishing a redemptive focus of ministry.

While there are many similarities represented in each model, their differences are quite stark in comparison. They all share in the same mission of fulfilling the Great Commission; however, the methods that they use vary based upon their mission, vision, and core values.

Faith Christian Worship Center's model of redemption focuses on discipleship, where the incremental growth of the new converts is the primary focus of the ministry. Under the leadership of Pastor Gary Johnson, the church's focus is to empower the disciple by training and developing them through the Word of God. A strategic discipleship plan is in place for the redemptive work of Jesus Christ to be active in the life of the believer. Once the new convert has acknowledged their desire to accept Jesus Christ as their Lord and Savior, they are invited to participate in a class entitled, "New Creation," which is based on the Apostle Paul's letter to the church of Corinth, "So if anyone is in Christ, there is a new creation: everything old has passed away; see, everything has become new."[3] The New Creation Class is a six-week class that focuses on understanding and comprehending your salvation. A 4-week class entitled, "Boot Camp," teaches the new disciple, the doctrine of the church and the process of sanctification, and it equips the new convert with the biblical and practical tools needed for their journey of discipleship following the New Creation Class.

---

[3] 2 Corinthians 5:17 NRSV

Greater Paradise is a charismatic church, where the culture of the church is a culture of empowerment and vision. The redemptive model of Greater Paradise is expressed through the practical work of the Word of God and through ministry encounters that focus on serving and empowering the community. The person and work of Jesus is the fuel that drives the momentum of the church. Greater Paradise's vision of a redemptive model is articulated through a vision entitled, "Vision 2020," where the church's desire is to create a center of hope in the heart of the community that serves as the hub of the community and houses all of the activities of an inner-city community and church. The activities would include a community resource center for economic empowerment, a recreation center for sports and the greater needs of the children and youth, and an entertainment complex that promotes family activities and engagement. This vision seeks to create a sense of belonging, which is vital to human flourishing as Julia Wood notes, "All of us need others to be happy, to enjoy life, to feel comfortable on the job, and to enrich experiences. We want others' company, acceptance, and affirmation, and we want to give acceptance and affirmation to others."[4] As a result, Greater Paradise views their method of ministry as a demonstration of the love of Christ through compassion and the realities of life.

Adams Chapel African Methodist Episcopal Church expresses their redemptive focus through the lens of the AMEC, which focuses on empowerment through discipleship and the social climate that impacts the African-American community. The vision of the founder of Adams Chapel was for the church to become magnetic, fulfilling the vision and mission of the church through the process of reproduction based on the teaching of the Great Commission:

And Jesus came and said to them, all authority in heaven and on earth has been given to me. Go therefore and make disciples of all nations, baptizing them in the name of the Father and of the Son and of the Holy Spirit, and teaching them to obey

---

[4] Julia T. Wood, *Interpersonal Communication: Everyday Encounters* (Belmont, CA: Wadsworth, 2002), 13.

everything that I have commanded you. And remember, I am with you always, to the end of the age.[5]

Dr. Thomas expressed that each member should be able to share his or her reason for coming to Christ. In the sharing, Dr. Thomas believes that the redemptive story will continue through the generations, a story that will provide life and construct an atmosphere for the progression of the church. Adams Chapel is a direct result of the power of reproduction. Bethel AME Church is one of the largest and most influential churches in the AMEC denomination. Out of their desire to reproduce themselves and further the greater purpose of the AMEC, they developed a strategic plan that focuses on reproduction. Adams Chapel is the byproduct of the church's desire to be faithful to the commands of Jesus and to establish a redemptive model for the AMEC.

All of the models presented have a desire in fulfilling the Great Commission even though their methods are very different. Their differences contribute greatly in establishing a redemptive

---

[5] Matthew 28:18-20 NRSV

model for church planting that will be beneficial to present generations and for generations to come. The aspects presented in the differences will be useful to the ongoing work of the church. Aspects such as denominational structure and influence, vision empowerment, and centered discipleship will aid the church planter in establishing an effective ministry.

Findings

How can church planting in the African-American context be redemptive for the African-American church? The question assumes that it wants to experience redemption and enrich its legacy and tradition across generations. In the case studies and pastoral interviews, our research question was answered in a myriad of ways. Each answer proves the validity of the subject of redemption. Redemption was expressed in every answer, strategic plan, ministry objective, mission statement, and vision. The theme of redemption is relevant and substantial for the ongoing work of the church. The primary focus of our definition of redemption is found within the Redemptive Model:

"competency, principles, character, and transformation"[6]. Our definition of redemption provides the stimulation and furthermore serves as a compass for the life and future of the African-American church. Within our ministry setting, redemption is embodied as a result of being "Catalysts for Life," defined as people determined to make someone's life better through the power and love of Jesus Christ.

As a result, the redemptive focus of our model is to be a catalyst of transformation and discipleship for both believers and non-believers by impacting countries, inspiring cultures, and influencing communities through the power and love of the gospel of Jesus Christ. This is demonstrated through a set of core values that provide the framework for the redemptive model:

---

[6] Drs. Claude R. Alexander and Rodney L. Cooper, "African-American Redemptive Leadership: Foundations and Development of Teams" (lecture, Gordon-Conwell Theological Seminary, Charlotte, NC, September 21, 2012).

1. Kingdom Values (Micah 6:8)
2. Kingdom Principles (Matthew 5:1-12)
3. Kingdom Living (Matthew 6:33-34)
4. Kingdom Witnessing (Acts 8:35-40)
5. Kingdom Building (Matthew 16:18-19)

As a result, the mission of redemption is to be an ambassador of hope, courage, and faith through the power of the gospel and the love of Jesus Christ. Our goal in the redemptive model is to bring people into a genuine relationship with God.

Therefore, the pastors and churches represented in each model strengthen our model and offer significant contributions to the further development of the redemptive model of church planting in the African-American context. Each model shares in the commonality of the salvation of Jesus Christ and the Great Commission, but each model also presents its own expression of how that work is embodied as a result of using our brokenness as a way to further our development in Christ.

The purpose of this project was to produce a working model that would serve as a redemptive model for church planters in the African-American context of ministry. The case study method was used in an effort to provide a multi-dimensional look at each pastor and their process of church planting. Our desire was for each case study to illustrate the significance of establishing a sustainable model of relevant and effective ministry.

As a result of the case studies, pastoral interviews, and questionnaires we discovered that each pastor represented had a heart for the Kingdom of God, and that their vision, strategies, and plans were affirmed by the Holy Spirit and supported by the faith community.

Suggestions for Future Studies

The goal of the project was to provide a comprehensive redemptive leadership model. Throughout our research, we discovered several suggestions for further development of the model. First, the focus of our project came directly from the pastors and the churches they were assigned to plant. In further development of this project, we would suggest interviewing members within those congregations as well those who represent the demographic of each faith community of the church in an effort to gain a balanced perspective of the church. As we continue to engage in the process, we would welcome another research method that would take a quantitative approach in an effort to get a broader range of data on the impact and effect of the aforementioned model. In addition, we would encourage another demographic to be investigated in the pursuit of establishing a redemptive model of church planting in the African-American context. Finally, this research method allows for an extensive examination of each church that would provide an opportunity for discussion and further examination of all churches looking to embrace a redemptive model.

Conclusion

In our efforts to be faithful to the will of God by fulfilling the Great Commission in an effort to establish the kingdom of God on earth as it is in heaven, we are encouraged to reflect on the progress that the African-American church has had on the world. During our time of reflection, we are invited to discipline ourselves with self-imposed measures in an effort to provide a culture of growth that will breathe life into the African-American church. Since the inception of the church, it has had a tremendous impact on the society at large; however, with that progress we are called to a greater level of demonstration that challenges our call and election. Furthermore, we believe that the redemptive model serves as a catalyst and as an invitation to further study of the substantial work and value that comes with the African-American church, a model that is beneficial in this present age as well as in the age to come.

APPENDIX A

PASTORAL INTERVIEWS

Dr. Michael O. Thomas, Founder of Adams Chapel A.M.E. Church

Criteria 1: Church planting pastors in the African-American context were selected to identify their personal vision of church planting.

1. What experiences have led you to church planting in the African-American context?
   I had no experiences. My pastor had no experiences. He encouraged me to speak with pastors in the city who had planted churches. AME Church had not started a church in Baltimore in 32 years. This is recorded in the AFRO, March 1982.

2. In your estimation, what is the current state of the African-American church?
   The current state of the AA church is that it is in the process of re-inventing its self. Young preachers male/female who are opposed to denominational regulations and restraints are leaving mainline denominations in large numbers to form their own congregations. Some have formal education while others do not. This education or lack may range from either "street knowledge" to lawyers, engineers or real estate agents.

3. When you hear the word "redemption" in relation to the African-American church, what are your thoughts?
   Preaching the gospel to save souls for Christ is my response.

4. How does the African-American church connect with younger generations and the surrounding cultures and communities?
   Many larger church starts are fortunate to hire a younger person to minister to their youth. These congregations break with the tradition of dressing for worship, meet at non-standard worship hours of Sunday. Many congregations include a Hip-Hop form of worship.

5. In your estimation, how is church planting viewed among established African-American pastors?
   It depends on how the church is planted. AA pastors of the traditional worship might view these emerging churches as cults, or social gatherings since they may use social networks to call people together.

6. What's your vision for a redemptive model in the African-American context?
   Each member should share his or her reason for coming to Christ.

Criteria 2: Church planting pastors in the African-American context were selected to identify the implementation of the vision of church planting in the African-American context.

1. How is your church implementating a vision of the Redemptive Model?
   Currently, pastoring an older congregation is a challenge for evangelism. Elders do not share their faith stories to others except in a 'canned testimony' setting that is told so often that the truth is difficult to parse.

2. How would the Redemptive Model of church planting in the African-American context, benefit the African-American church and community?
   I think most black preachers use some form of the redemptive model. The ones that are extraordinarily popular and unusual reveal growth is in my estimation due to the personality of the preacher.

3. What's your theological rationale for church planting in the African-American context?
   Matthew 28:18-20

4. How can the traditional African-American church and the Redemptive Model of church planting complement one another?
   It may be accomplished by interactivity of beliefs.

5. In your estimation, what's the future of the African-American church?
   Over time the redemptive model will become the new AA church as the baby-boomers generation dies off.

Criteria 3: Church planting pastors in the African-American context were selected to share their results and experience of church planting in the African-American context.

1. How has your church progressed as a church plant in the African-American context?
   I pastored Adam's Chapel for only 3 years as its founder. However, 32 years later the church is still progressing.

2. What are the significant benchmarks that you would identify in the success and stability of the church?
   Unable to answer this question and number 3.

3. What's the external perception of the church among the surrounding communities?

4. What if anything would you do differently as a church planter?
   Under a bishop controlled denomination it was not possible to do much else.

5. As a result of your experience, what would you identify as key themes in church planting in the African-American context?

Preaching

Music

Teaching

Youth Ministry

Pastor Gary Johnson, Founder and Pastor of Faith Christian Worship Center

Criteria 1: Church planting pastors in the African-American context were selected to identify their personal vision of church planting.

1. What experiences have led you to church planting in the African-American context?

   My experiences of dealing with low-income people, growing up in the projects, not having my Father

2. In your estimation, what is the current state of the African-American church?

   A church that's not fully committed to Jesus Christ, Newer Generation, "Nothing is Sacred."

3. When you hear the word "redemption" in relation to the African-American church, what are your thoughts?

We have a partnership with Jesus; church is a part of the plan to win the world for Jesus.

4. How does the African-American church connect with younger generations and the surrounding cultures and communities?
   Being in their face, being present in the community.

5. In your estimation, how is church planting viewed among established African-American pastors?
   Church planting is viewed as alternative for those who didn't qualify for established churches. Church planters are viewed as "disgruntled" with infrastructure and rebels.

6. What's your vision for a redemptive model in the African-American context? Outlined on the Website

Criteria 2: Church planting pastors in the African-American context were selected to identify the implementation of the vision of church planting in the African-American context.

1. How is your church implanting a vision of the Redemptive Model?
   Foundation is the word of God, once they join the ministry. New Creation Class (4 week), followed by Boot Camp (6 weeks) as they are taught doctrine, justification and sanctification. Followed by mandatory weekly bible study.

2. How would the Redemptive Model of church planting in the African-American context, benefit the African-American church and community?

   Greatly, we need more redemptive models. The Gospel needs to be spread = New Churches Everywhere.

3. What's your theological rationale for church planting in the African-American context?

   Great Commission = Matthew 28:16-20

4. How can the traditional African-American church and the Redemptive Model of church planting complement one another?

   Traditional church taking the lead and being a big brother, father figure, instead of looking down on the work of the church planter.

5. In your estimation, what's the future of the African-American church?

   Great Future, God is with us! Greater impact for the Kingdom.

Criteria 3: Church planting pastors in the African-American context were selected to share their results and experience of church planting in the African-American context.

1. How has your church progressed as a church plant in the African-American context?

    Within 17 years, since the inception of our church, the people of the church have progressed spiritually, emotionally and physically. They started off low-income with no jobs, 80percent of the members have quality jobs and have move from renters to home ownership. Great increase and self-sufficient.

2. What are the significant benchmarks that you would identify in the success and stability of the church?

    The Word of God being active in the life of the church has been the primary benchmark. Stability.

3. What's the external perception of the church among the surrounding communities?

    They are different, they are loving, and they are willing to come where we are.

4. What if anything would you do differently as a church planter?

    Believe in the vision from the inception, less doubting and more faith in God. Not despising the day of small beginnings.

5. As a result of your experience, what would you identify as key themes in church planting in the African-American context?
Believing in the Vision, Vision Team, Strategic Planning, Word of God, Knowing Your Culture.

Pastor Shawn Bell, Founder and Pastor of Greater Paradise Christian Center

Criteria 1: Church planting pastors in the African-American context were selected to identify their personal vision of church planting.

1. What experiences have led you to church planting in the African-American context?
Exposure at young age to see outside of the denomination, and various models of ministry. (Relational)

2. In your estimation, what is the current state of the African-American church?
Trouble, many of the churches operate in a slavery mindset, fail to embrace the 21st century model. Divided...

3. When you hear the word "redemption" in relation to the African-American church, what are your thoughts?
Restoration, integrity, revival.

4. How does the African-American church connect with younger generations and the surrounding cultures and communities?

Inclusive of culture, we are in the world, but not of the world. Being relevant, to social issues, political, (don't preach it, produce it).

5. In your estimation, how is church planting viewed among established African-American pastors?
Poor Reception, Cautious. No one introduced you! Extend the Olive Branch!

6. What's your vision for a redemptive model in the African-American context?
Vision 20/20 create a center of hope that will house all of the activities of the inner-city community, for the purpose that people will be saved in the name of Jesus Christ.

Criteria 2: Church planting pastors in the African-American context were selected to identify the implementation of the vision of church planting in the African-American context.

1. How is your church implementing a vision of the Redemptive Model?
Preach the vision; invest time and resources into the vision, parent and child relationship.

2. How would the Redemptive Model of church planting in the African-American context, benefit the African-American church and community?

Establish a relevant context that will benefit the legacy of generations to follow.

3. What's your theological rationale for church planting in the African-American context?

   Christ-Centered, he didn't establish churches, but there were churches on foot that sets the framework of what church planting should look like.

4. How can the traditional African-American church and the Redemptive Model of church planting complement one another?

   Obtaining structure, passing of the guard, balance.

5. In your estimation, what's the future of the African-American church?

   Remain the church, the next generation, concern to keep its power and truth. Heighten level of concern. Intergenerational connection that it will take to preserve.

Criteria 3: Church planting pastors in the African-American context were selected to share their results and experience of church planting in the African-American context.

1. How has your church progressed as a church plant in the African-American context?

   Sustainability, the biggest testament.

2. What are the significant benchmarks that you would identify in the success and stability of the church?

   Fire, tragedy, sustainability. Redemption (benchmarks) foundation. Business affairs, insurance. Strong infrastructure. The new pastor needs to be equipped to manage the church (administrator).

3. What's the external perception of the church among the surrounding communities?

   Non-Denominational, but refers to as Pentecostal.

4. What if anything would you do differently as a church planter?

   Decision-making, membership retention, and financial mistakes. Overpaid staff.

5. As a result of your experience, what would you identify as key themes in church planting in the African-American context of ministry?

   Community Relations, Relationships

APPENDIX B
MARKETING STRATEGIES WORKSHOP FOR THE CHURCH PLANTER

1 Dream Big

Embrace your dream through prayer and the development of your vision. Pray to seek clarity on your event meeting the overall vision of the house. Your individual dream may not always be meant for the house.

2 Crew Call

Find your crew and develop your team. Get three or four individuals that have abilities to contribute to your team. They should be outgoing, familiar with technology, willing to think out of the box (innovative/risk takers), and have a good grasp of grammar and the English language.

3 Production Planning

Create your production schedule and develop your timeline. Plan accordingly while weighing the risk and outcome for each task, then prioritize, prioritize, prioritize!

4 The Nielsen Sample

Do some market research to know your audience and their demographics. Understand to whom you are marketing and why. For example, if you are creating an event for women, know the age range and the type of woman you are targeting. Then, ask women about women—learn what women like to do and what visually appeals to them.

5 Production Enhancements

Make your production look good. Improve your image and event through branding. Define yourself, your house, and your event through a clear, consistent, and constant presence. Know who you are and own it.

6 The Art of the Spin

Use the media to spin your story in a positive direction. Before you pay for expensive marketing campaigns, exhaust your options with free social media. Market your event on Facebook, LinkedIn, Twitter, YouTube, and Pinterest. However, you cannot forget the value of marketing through word-of-mouth and at local venues such as the salon or the barbershop. You are guaranteed a greater return on your print ad monies by using "good ole fashion" alternatives for getting the word out!

7 Stylists

Find people that will make you look your best. Identify two or more reliable graphic designers. They must have a great eye for advertising and be able to complete quick fulfillments (turnarounds) on print ads.

8 The Paparazzi

Be kind to all media personnel from the production assistant to the executive directors. Media relations can make or break your image. This is a critical relationship for any modern day charismatic pastor. It is essential to either know radio, TV, or print (magazine) personalities, or know someone who knows them well. These types of relationships, whether you are a business or church leader, can prove to be highly beneficial.

Elder Shawn Bell
Pastor of Greater Paradise Christian Center • Baltimore, Maryland www.greaterparadise.org

Appendix C

The Nine Fruits of Finance

Educating, Equipping & Empowering Individuals Seeking to Develop Extraordinary Finance
The Foundation of Stewardship....

John 15:5NKJV
"I am the vine, you are the branches. He who abides in Me, and I in him, bears much fruit; for without Me you can do nothing."

Financial Stewardship & Discipline is the key to understanding and accepting our role; we are God's stewards *first*. Our lives, talents, gifts, abilities, and living in a world of unprecedented, unequal unparalleled and unmatched opportunities are all gifts granted from God. The Nine Fruits of Finance were developed to assist in gaining a new financial appreciation for the truth:

Acts 17:28
NKJV
"For in him we live, and move, and have our being".

The Nine Financial Fruits were designed to address the intangible emotional connections associated with finances — intangible emotional connections much like the nine Fruits of the Spirit. While we cannot touch, feel, smell, hear or taste the fruit, when they are present, we know of their existence. Our ultimate purpose and desire is to identify and release the real or imaginary strongholds so that we may foster an environment of financial trust built on rational decision making skills.

Financial Stewardship requires extraordinary faith and trust in God. However, one must Level Set with Their Mindset, Themselves and Their Finances to effectively execute and sustain the discipline of Financial Stewardship.

The Nine Fruits of Finance workshops Educates, Equips and Empowers individuals with hands on life skills and grass roots applications designed to assist in the maturation of one's giving approach thus, Developing Extraordinary Financial Stewardship by...

Defeating Financial Fears

FINANCIAL FEAR & FAITH: Facing Fears through Filtered Faith

Financial Fear has the potential to be a very powerful emotional distraction. The Fruits of Financial Fear & Faith will allow you to "dive deep" into the most common financial fears experienced by many, identify their root causes, and defeat your fears by the execution of filtered faith.

Accepting Financial Accountability

FINANCIAL AWARENESS & ACCOUNTABILITY: Admittance, Acceptance & Action

Nothing changes unless something changes. Financial Awareness & Accountability is an essential step in facing your financial fears and the beginning of financial transformation and freedom. These fruits will allow you to view your financial condition; assets, liabilities, income, expenses and net worth in a robust workshop designed to educate, equip and empower you through the use of a Personal Financial Statement.

Identifying Financial Streams

FINANCIAL SOURCES & STREAMS: Identifying what's in your hands?

What are your Gifts? What are your Talents? The Fruits of Sources & Streams seeks to assist in identifying the gifts, talents, dreams and desires that are buried deep within. Once identified, we will breathe life into your Gifts & Talents by introducing the 10 Steps of Starting a Business and the 7 Steps of Writing a Business Plan.

Plugging Financial Leaks

FINANCIAL LEAKS & LOADS: How do we PLUG & SEAL them?

What's draining your finances? Financial leaks are threats that may affect your ability to control your finances and budget accordingly. Financial loads are the excess financial burdens that tend to weigh you down and are a distraction to financial goal achievement. We will discuss where to look for both financial leaks and loads and discuss structured processes to PLUG & SEAL them permanently.

Repairing Financial Conditions

FINANCIAL REPAIR &REDEMPTION: Restoring the Broke & Broken

Even if you have been through an economic crisis, all is not lost. Credit grading is based on so many factors. We will discuss: The 4 C's of Credit, The Credit Cycle, Strategies to improve Credit Quality, Pros & Cons of Borrowing, your Rights as a Borrower and so much more. *Financial Repair & Redemption is the introduction to Financial Discipline & Discipleship.*

Improving Financial Discipline

FINANCIAL DISCIPLINE & DISCIPLESHIP: *Knowing what to "Offer Up"*

The Fruits of Discipline & Discipleship will assist you in identifying key resources and explore ways of utilizing them to improve your outlook and ability to plan for the financial future you desire. We will discuss the discipline required to establish a Personal Budget and set incremental financial goals. Once effectively implemented, the charge is to be a disciple of your knowledge and efforts.

Discovering Financial Contentment

FINANCIAL COURAGE, COMMITMENT & CONTENTMENT*: Recognizing the "New Norm"*

The "Three C's" will address the vision you have for your financial success, the path to obtain financial success and mindset to appreciate and celebrate the financial success you have achieved. Your new financial behaviors are now your "New Norm" which will shape your financial decisions, thus allowing you the boldness required to substitute emotional financial thinking for rational financial thinking. What does the "New You" look like?

Releasing Financial Empowerment

FINANCIAL EXECUTION & EMPOWERMENT: *Activating your Plan of Action*

Writing down your financial goals converts them into a plan and not just a dream. We will discuss how to prepare an Effective Performance Action Plan which will include the SMART- ER model. We will host an Objection Clinic in anticipation of any likely unforeseen obstacles and/or challenges; seek steps to overcome; and discuss ways to avoid any future financial pitfalls.

Obtaining & Sustaining Financial Freedom

FINANCIAL FREEDOM & FUTURE: *Quality vs. Quantity — A Lifetime Choice*

Your financial Freedom & Future is "your" choice. It's about looking forward to seeing yourself and your family live a well-balanced quality life; financially, physically and emotionally. Financial Freedom & Future focuses on sustained peace and prosperity. Financial Planning tools will be introduced as you seek to establish and protect your family's inheritance and/or your legacy.

At Fruits of Finance we firmly believe in helping people and organizations prosper. We possess a passion and drive for developing others to achieve their personal and professional goals by empowering, equipping and educating those seeking to Develop Extra-Ordinary Finances. My extensive professional background and personal experiences have afforded me the ability to teach foundational financial principles through workshops based on The Nine Fruits of Finance. I "aspires to inspire" in all of my professional, spiritual, and personal interactions.

JaNean Stubbs-Taylor
CEO & Founder of The Nine Fruits of Finance* Westminster, MD www.fruitsoffinance.org

BIBLIOGRAPHY

"African-American Church Planting Research Report," LifeWay Research, last modified July 15, 2013, accessed November 10, 2013, http://pcamna.org/wordpress/wp-content/uploads/2013/08/African-American-Church-Planting-Final-Quantitative- Research-Report.pdf

Anyabwile, Thabiti M. *The Decline of African American Theology*. Downers Grove, IL: InterVarsity, 2007.

Arnold, Clinton E. ed. *Zondervan Illustrated Bible Background Commentary*. Vol.1, *Matthew, Mark, Luke,* Grand Rapids, MI: Zondervan, 2002.

Baird, William. "The Acts of Jesus in Galilee", *The Interpreter's One-Volume Commentary on the Bible,* ed. Charles M. Layman, 681. Nashville, TN: Abingdon Press, 1971.

Barclay, William. *The Gospel of Luke*. Louisville, KY: Westminster John Knox Press, 2001.

Barna, George and Harry R. Jackson. *High Impact African-American Churches*. Ventura, CA: Regal Books, 2004.

Blomberg, Craig L. *Jesus and the Gospels*. Nashville, TN: Broadman & Holman Publishers,1997.

Bock, Darrell L. *Luke*. Downers Grove, IL: InterVaristy Press, 1994.

Bovon, Francois. *A Commentary on the Gospel of Luke 1:1-9:50*, Hermeneia: A Critical & Historical Commentary on the Bible. Minneapolis, MN: Fortress Press, 2002.

Bruce, F.F. *Zondervan Bible Commentary*. Grand Rapids, MI: Zondervan, 2008.

Buttrick, George. *The Interpreter's One-Volume Commentary on the Bible*. Nashville, TN: Abingdon Press, 1971.

Chambers, Oswald. *Growing Deeper With God*. Ann Arbor, MI: Servant Publications, 1997.

Collins, Jim. *Good to Great*. New York, NY: Harper Business, 2001.

Conn, Harvie. *Planting & Growing Urban Churches*. Grand Rapids, MI: Baker Books, 2002.

Cooper, Rodney L. *Holman New Testament Commentary*. Nashville, TN: Broadman & Holman Reference, 2000.

Cosgrove, Charles H., Herold D. Weiss, and Khiok-Khng Yeo. *Cross-Cultural Paul: Journeys to Others, Journeys to Ourselves.* Grand Rapids, MI: Wm. B. Eerdmans, 2005.

Cox, Michael J., and Joe Samuel Ratliff. *Church Planting in the African-American Community.* Valley Forge, PA: Judson Press, 2002.

Craddock, Fred B. *Luke.* Louisville, KY: Westminster John Knox Press, 1990.

Erickson, Millard J. *Introducing Christian Doctrine.* Grand Rapids, MI: Baker Academic, 2001.

Fitzmyer, Joseph *The Gospel According to Luke I-IX,* vol. 28, *Anchor Bible.* New York, NY: Doubleday & Company, 1981.

Flake, Floyd H., and Elaine McCollins Flake. *African American Church Management Handbook.* Valley Forge, PA: Judson, Press, 2005.

Francis, Hozell C. *Church Planting in the African-American Context.* Grand Rapids, MI: Zondervan Publishing, 1999.

Green, Joel B. *The Gospel of Luke.* Grand Rapids, MI: Wm. B. Eerdmans Publishing Company, 1997.

Griffith, Jim and Bill Easum. *Ten Most Common Mistakes Among Church Planters*. St. Louis, MO: Chalice Press, 2008.

Hamilton, Adam. *Leading Beyond the Walls*. Nashville, TN: Abingdon Press, 2002.

Hammond, John S. "Learning by the Case Method," *Harvard Business School*, April 16, 2002, http://sphweb.bumc.bu.du/otlt/teachingLibrary/Case20Teaching/learning-by-case-method.pdf

Hutchinson, Orion N., Jr. *Basic Bible Commentary* vol. 19, *Luke*. Nashville, TN: Abingdon Press, 1988.

Jones, Major J. *The Color of God: The Concept of God in Afro-American Thought*. Macon, GA: Mercer University Press, 1990.

Keener, Craig S. *The Bible Background Commentary*. Downers Grove, IL: Intervarsity Press, 1993.

Lewis, Candace. "Things to Consider in New Church Planting in African American Context," accessed November, 14, 2013, http://www.path1.org/images/File/AA%20Church%20planting%20best%20practices%2006_07_10.pdf.

Lincoln, C. Eric and Lawrence H. Mamiya. *The Black Church in the African American Experience*. Durham, NC: Duke University Press, 1990.

Lumsden, Gary and Donald Lumsden. *Communicating in Groups & Teams*. Belmont, CA: Wadsworth/Thompson Learning, 2000.

Malphurs, Aubrey. *Advanced Strategic Planning: A New Model for Church & Ministry Leaders*. Grand Rapids, MI: Baker Books, 1999.

———. *Planting Growing Churches for the 21st Century*. Grand Rapids, MI: Baker Books, 1998.

———. *The Nuts and Bolts of Church Planting: A Guide for starting any kind of Church*. Grand Rapids, MI: Baker Books, 2011.

Maxwell, John C. *Winning with People*. Nashville, TN: Nelson Books, 2004.

McIntosh, Gary. *One Church, Four Generations: Understanding and Reaching All Ages in Your Church*. Grand Rapids, MI: Baker Books, 2002.

Meeks, Wayne A. *The First Urban Christians*. New Haven, CT: Yale University Press, 2003.

Migliore, Daniel L. *Faith Seeking Understanding*. Grand Rapids, MI: William B. Eerdmans Publishing Company, 2004.

Moore, Ralph. *Starting a New Church*. Ventura, CA: Regal Books, 2002.

Nebel, Tom and Gary Rohrmayer. *Church Planting Landmines.* Saint Charles, IL: Church Smart Resources, 2005.

Nelson, Alan E. *Spirituality & Leadership.* Colorado Springs, CO: NavPress, 2002.

Peterson, Eugene H. *Christ Plays in Ten Thousand Places.* Grand Rapids, MI: William B. Eerdmans Publishing Company, 2005.

Phillips, John. *Exploring the Gospel of Luke.* Grand Rapids, MI: Kregel Publications, 2005.

Pringle, Paul. *You the Leader.* New Kensington, PA: Whitaker House, 2005.

Proctor, Samuel D., and Gardner C. Taylor. *We Have This Ministry.* Valley Forge, PA: Judson Press, 1996.

Roetzel, Calvin J. *The Letters of Paul.* Louisville, KY: Westminster John Knox Press, 1998.

Russell, Bob. *When God Builds A Church.* West Monroe, LA: Howard Publishing, 2000.

Scazzero, Peter. *The Emotionally Healthy Church.* Grand Rapids, MI: Zondervan, 2010.

Sider, Ronald, Philip N. Olson, and Heidi Rolland Unruh. *Churches That Make a Difference.* Grand Rapids, MI: Baker Books, 2006.

Schaller, Lyle E. *44 Questions for Church Planters.* Nashville, TN: Abingdon Press, 1991.

Sernett, Milton C. *African American Religious History: A Documentary Witness.* Durham, NC: Duke University Press, 1999.

Stetzer, Ed. "African-American Church Planting," *Christianity Today*, September 4, 2013, http://www.christianitytoday.com/edstetzer/2013/september/new-research-on-african-american-church-planting.html.

———. "Observations and Implications of African American Church Planting," *Christianity Today*, July 25, 2013, http://www.christianitytoday.com/edstetzer/2013/july/observations-and-implications-of-african-american-church-pl.html.

———. *Planting Missional Churches.* Nashville, TN: Broadman & Holman Publishers, 2006.

Vernon, R.A. *Size Does Matter.* Cleveland, OH: Victory Media & Publishing Company, 2011.

Williams, Ronald C. *Serving God with Style.* Bethesda, MD: Alban Institute Publication, 2002.

Williamson, Lamar, Jr. *Mark*. Louisville, KY: Westminster John Knox Press, 1973.

Wood, Julia T. *Interpersonal Communication: Everyday Encounters*. Belmont, CA: Wadsworth, 2002.

Wright, Tom. *Luke for Everyone*. Louisville, KY: Westminster John Knox Press, 2004.

Yin, Robert K. *Case Study Research: Design and Methods*. Thousand Oaks, CA: Sage Publications, 2003.

VITA

Jermaine Nathaniel Johnson
Baltimore, Maryland

Eastern University   2001-2004
Bachelor of Arts, Relational Communication

Northern Seminary   2005-2007
Masters of Divinity, Pastoral Care/Leadership Development

Gordon Conwell Theological Seminary 2010-2014
Doctor of Ministry, Redemptive Leadership

Honors and Awards:
Wesley Theological Seminary
Lewis Fellows   2013-2014

Kenilworth Union Church
Bi-Centennial Scholar 2006-2009

Northern Seminary
Ian Chapman Leadership Award 2007

Melvin James Battle Scholarship Recipient 2006

Message from the Author:

The Content within this book is designed to help cultivate and facilitate a process of leadership development as well as provide an atmosphere to establish a leadership model within your context of ministry.

"Every new church needs a leadership culture...no longer will you pray for God to bring you leaders, because leadership development will become normal and effective in your new church."

It's my prayer that as you read this book and embrace the content within that your church and ministry will truly experience a sense of fulfillment as you gain greater insight in your leadership and service to the Kingdom of God.

Dr. Jermaine N. Johnson
Jermaine Johnson Ministries, LLC

Additional Resources:
The Wine Experience Workbook $10.00
The New Wine Experience Workbook serves as a catalyst to the book.

Contact Information:
Dr. Jermaine N. Johnson
(443) 744-7869
P.O Box 16
Owings Mills, Maryland 21117

Download the App:
Jermaine Johnson Ministries
Email: DrJohnson317@gmail.com
www.wolccc.org